"Dr. Lori Reichel is an expert in her field. She understands that children need to self-regulate before they can learn. She has skillfully compiled this resource book with multiple tools that are practical, easy to use activities which will benefit both student and teacher. Emotionally regulated children focus, learn, retain, and ultimately feel better about themselves. Learning these lifelong emotional regulation skills will benefit them now and throughout their adult lives."

**Dr. Kelli Palfy**, *Registered Psychologist, Alberta, Canada*

# Tactile Tools for Social Emotional Learning

Many emotional learning activities – the "E" in Social Emotional Learning (SEL) – include self-regulation skills typically led by teachers, but why not empower young people by giving them tools to choose their own self-regulation techniques? This practical and comprehensive book features 52 activities focusing on emotional learning, specifically self-regulation skills that incorporate tactile objects students can store in their personal "toolboxes." Each activity can be taught or guided by a teacher or classroom leader, supporting children to take charge of their own feelings and behavior, and thereby their own learning success. *Tactile Tools for Social Emotional Learning* is an important addition to any teacher's toolkit and is key reading for early childhood educators, elementary school teachers, resource/SPED teachers, and pre-service teachers.

**Lori A. Reichel, PhD**, is an Assistant Professor at SUNY Cortland and a health education consultant. She has taught health education, including SEL, for over 30 years, teaching every grade in the K-12 setting. Due to her expertise, Lori has received many awards, including the New York State AHPERD Health Teacher of the Year (2007), the Eastern Division AHPERD Health Teacher of the Year (2009), the National AHPERD Professional of the Year Award in Health Education (2010), and the New York State AHPERD Professional of the Year Award in 2011.

## Other Eye on Education Books Available from Routledge
(www.routledge.com/eyeoneducation)

**Everyday SEL in Elementary School**
Integrating Social Emotional Learning and Mindfulness Into Your Classroom, Second Edition
*Carla Tantillo Philibert*

**Everyday SEL in Early Childhood**
Integrating Social Emotional Learning and Mindfulness Into Your Classroom, Second Edition
*Carla Tantillo Philibert*

**The Flexible SEL Classroom**
Practical Ways to Build Social Emotional Learning, Second Edition
*Amber Chandler*

**Relational Inclusivity in the Elementary Classroom**
A Teacher's Guide to Supporting Student Friendships and Building Nurturing Communities
*Christoforos Mamas, Shana R. Cohen, and Caren Holtzman*

# Tactile Tools for Social Emotional Learning

## Activities to Help Children Self-Regulate with SEL, PreK-5

Lori A. Reichel

Routledge
Taylor & Francis Group
NEW YORK AND LONDON

Designed cover image: © Getty Images

First published 2025
by Routledge
605 Third Avenue, New York, NY 10158

and by Routledge
4 Park Square, Milton Park, Abingdon, Oxon, OX14 4RN

*Routledge is an imprint of the Taylor & Francis Group, an informa business*

© 2025 Taylor & Francis

The right of Lori A. Reichel to be identified as author of this work has been asserted in accordance with sections 77 and 78 of the Copyright, Designs and Patents Act 1988.

All rights reserved. The purchase of this copyright material confers the right on the purchasing institution to photocopy pages which bear the photocopy icon and copyright line at the bottom of the page. No other parts of this book may be reprinted or reproduced or utilised in any form or by any electronic, mechanical, or other means, now known or hereafter invented, including photocopying and recording, or in any information storage or retrieval system, without permission in writing from the publishers.

*Trademark notice*: Product or corporate names may be trademarks or registered trademarks, and are used only for identification and explanation without intent to infringe.

ISBN: 9781032903194 (hbk)
ISBN: 9781032903170 (pbk)
ISBN: 9781003547051 (ebk)

DOI: 10.4324/9781003547051

Typeset in Palatino
by codeMantra

*For teachers, parents, and other caregivers
who continue to help young people
be as healthy as they can be.*

# Contents

*Meet the Author* . . . . . . . . . . . . . . . . . . . . . . . . . . . . . . . . . xiii

**Notes to the Teacher** . . . . . . . . . . . . . . . . . . . . . . . . . . . . . 1
What This Book Is About . . . . . . . . . . . . . . . . . . . . . . . . . 1
How This Book Is Different . . . . . . . . . . . . . . . . . . . . . . . 2
Who This Book Is For . . . . . . . . . . . . . . . . . . . . . . . . . . . . 4
Why This Book Was Written . . . . . . . . . . . . . . . . . . . . . . 5
Educational Best Practices and Standards . . . . . . . . . . . . . . 7
Creating a Positive Classroom Culture . . . . . . . . . . . . . . . . 10
Basic Terminology . . . . . . . . . . . . . . . . . . . . . . . . . . . . . . 15
Additional Resources . . . . . . . . . . . . . . . . . . . . . . . . . . . 19

**Getting Started** . . . . . . . . . . . . . . . . . . . . . . . . . . . . . . . . 21
Basic Recommendations . . . . . . . . . . . . . . . . . . . . . . . . . 21
Other Times SEL Tools Can Be Used . . . . . . . . . . . . . . . . 25
How the SEL Tools and Activities Are Presented . . . . . . . . 26
How Each SEL Tool and Activity Is Organized . . . . . . . . . 26

**A  Tools for Breathing and Awareness Activities** . . . . . . . . . 29
Tips for How to Use the SEL Tools in Section A . . . . . . . . . 29
Activity A1: Belly Breathing with a Hand . . . . . . . . . . . . . . 31
Activity A2: Breathing Out Bubbles . . . . . . . . . . . . . . . . . . 34
Activity A3: Listening Awareness . . . . . . . . . . . . . . . . . . . 36
Activity A4: Pinwheel Breathing . . . . . . . . . . . . . . . . . . . . 39
Activity A5: Smile Breathing . . . . . . . . . . . . . . . . . . . . . . 41
Activity A6: Sparkly Bottle Breathing . . . . . . . . . . . . . . . . 43
Activity A7: Belly Breathing with a Block . . . . . . . . . . . . . . 45
Activity A8: Body Scanning . . . . . . . . . . . . . . . . . . . . . . . 48
Activity A9: Box Breathing . . . . . . . . . . . . . . . . . . . . . . . . 52
Activity A10: Clouds as Our Thoughts Activity . . . . . . . . . . 56
Activity A11: Foot Awareness Activity . . . . . . . . . . . . . . . . 59

  Activity A12: Lazy Figure 8 Breathing . . . . . . . . . . . . . . . . . . 62
  Activity A13: Loving Kindness Activity . . . . . . . . . . . . . . . . 65
  Activity A14: String of Beads Centering Activity . . . . . . . . 67
  Activity A15: Triangle Breathing . . . . . . . . . . . . . . . . . . . . . . 69
  Activity A16: Breathing as a Flying Bird . . . . . . . . . . . . . . . 72
  Activity A17: Finding Our Center in 5 4 3 2 1 . . . . . . . . . . . 76
  Activity A18: Loving Body Scan . . . . . . . . . . . . . . . . . . . . . . 80
  Activity A19: Moving a Paper clip on a Thread . . . . . . . . . 84
  Activity A20: Parasympathetic "Reset" Breathing . . . . . . . 87
  Activity A21: Progressive Muscle Relaxation Practice . . . . . 90
  Activity A22: Slow Straw Breathing . . . . . . . . . . . . . . . . . . . 95

**B** **Other Sensory Tools** . . . . . . . . . . . . . . . . . . . . . . . . . . . . . . . . 97
  Tips for How to Use the SEL Tools in Section B . . . . . . . . . 97
  Activity B1: Chenille Fidgets . . . . . . . . . . . . . . . . . . . . . . . . 99
  Activity B2: Clay . . . . . . . . . . . . . . . . . . . . . . . . . . . . . . . . . 101
  Activity B3: Favorite Photo/Drawing . . . . . . . . . . . . . . . . 103
  Activity B4: Sock Puppet . . . . . . . . . . . . . . . . . . . . . . . . . . 105
  Activity B5: Yoga Cards . . . . . . . . . . . . . . . . . . . . . . . . . . . 107
  Activity B6: Favorite Scents . . . . . . . . . . . . . . . . . . . . . . . . 110
  Activity B7: Rain Stick . . . . . . . . . . . . . . . . . . . . . . . . . . . . 112
  Activity B8: Reminders of Nature . . . . . . . . . . . . . . . . . . . 115
  Activity B9: Slime . . . . . . . . . . . . . . . . . . . . . . . . . . . . . . . . 117
  Activity B10: Soft Noodle . . . . . . . . . . . . . . . . . . . . . . . . . . 119
  Activity B11: Stress Ball . . . . . . . . . . . . . . . . . . . . . . . . . . . 121
  Activity B12: Decider Origami . . . . . . . . . . . . . . . . . . . . . . 123
  Activity B13: Labyrinth . . . . . . . . . . . . . . . . . . . . . . . . . . . 128
  Activity B14: Laughter Tool . . . . . . . . . . . . . . . . . . . . . . . . 131

**C** **Tools Dealing With Words** . . . . . . . . . . . . . . . . . . . . . . . . . . 133
  Tips for How to Use the SEL Tools in Section C . . . . . . . . 133
  Activity C1: Feeling Cards . . . . . . . . . . . . . . . . . . . . . . . . . 135
  Activity C2: Gratitude Heart . . . . . . . . . . . . . . . . . . . . . . . 139
  Activity C3: Personal Support Hand . . . . . . . . . . . . . . . . 142
  Activity C4: "I am" Acrostic . . . . . . . . . . . . . . . . . . . . . . . . 145
  Activity C5: "I feel" Statements . . . . . . . . . . . . . . . . . . . . . 148
  Activity C6: Positive Reminders on a Stone . . . . . . . . . . . 154
  Activity C7: Erasing Thoughts . . . . . . . . . . . . . . . . . . . . . 156

Activity C8: Inspirational Words.......................158
Activity C9: Lessons Learned When Mistakes Happen...161
Activity C10: Letter to Myself........................164
Activity C11: Lil' Box of Worries.....................167
Activity C12: My Little Journal.......................170
Activity C13: Personal Mission Statement..............172
Activity C14: Positive Words For and From Others......174
Activity C15: Ten (10) Dreams.........................177
Activity C16: "Thank You" Note........................179

# Meet the Author

**Lori A. Reichel, PhD,** is a nationally recognized health educator with over 30 years of teaching experience. Recipient of the National Health Education Professional of the Year Award (2010) and NYS Health Education Teacher of the Year Award (2007), Lori currently trains future and current health education teachers at SUNY Cortland. Due to her passion for helping teachers and families be the best resources they can for children and youth, she created the School Health Educators Podcast in 2024, produced the Puberty Prof Podcast (2021–2023), authored *Common Questions Children Ask About Puberty*, and co-authored *Tools for Teaching Comprehensive Human Sexuality: Lessons, Activities, and Teaching Strategies Utilizing the National Sexuality Education Standards*. Lori lives with her husband and her Maltipoo in upstate New York where they explore the beautiful waterfalls and hiking trails to support their own social and emotional regulation.

You can refer to Lori's work, as well as her consulting services, on her websites www.lorireichel.com and www.schoolhealtheducators.org, or email her at superhealthcrusader@gmail.com.

# Notes to the Teacher

Social Emotional Learning (SEL) is a concept that resonates with many educators and school leaders. The book *Tactile Tools for Social Emotional Learning* aims to assist in the instruction of SEL to students in grades PreK-5 by offering tactile tools for them to utilize during self-regulation activities.

To best support your success, read the information in this section and the "Getting Started" section before referring to the provided SEL Tools and their corresponding activities. In this section you will find information on:

- What This Book Is About
- How This Book Is Different
- Who This Book Is For
- Why this Book Was Written
- Educational Best Practices and Standards
- Creating a Positive Classroom Culture
- Basic Terminology
- Additional Resources

## What This Book Is About

*Tactile Tools for Social Emotional Learning* provides the steps for helping students create SEL Tools to be stored in their own personal SEL Toolbox. These tools are tactile objects to help students complete a specific activity, fidget with, or be reminded of something positive.

Just like many households have a toolbox with tools to fix or build things, the tools referred to in this book are simple items to help build self-regulatory skills supporting students' emotional wellness. Most tools are associated with tactile objects students can hold in their hands, with some tools being made with pieces of paper or cardstock.

The purpose behind these tools and activities is to help young people:

- pause for a few moments to reflect and/or refocus,
- build their resiliency skills to work through challenges,
- identify how they feel,
- lower cortisol levels, a hormone in the body associated with distress,
- release healthy hormones, including serotonin, endorphins, and dopamine,
- shift how they see themselves in a challenging situation, and
- better understand themselves, including how their bodies respond to stress.

Remember these tools will not remove stress, especially because stress is a part of life. Instead, these tools support students' wellness by reminding them to pause, take a breath, complete a simple activity, and/or remember who they choose to be.

**Disclosure:** The information found in this book is solely for educational purposes and does not substitute professional medical advice. Please refer to qualified professionals, including medical doctors, to support the wellness of the young people in your life as well as yourself.

## How This Book Is Different

Many books and other resources are attempting to help young people with SEL. So what makes *Tactile Tools for Social Emotional Learning* different?

1. The tools referred to in this book have a *hands-on* or *tactile* aspect. By having something concrete (tactile) to hold onto and/or look at, referred to as a "tool," students are reminded to pause or complete an activity related to the item. Many of these tactile tools are made with cardstock paper or other inexpensive materials.

    *Note:* Due to the increased use of technology, young people are accustomed to holding a tablet or phone in their hands. The SEL Tools mentioned in this book support the habit of holding items that are *not* forms of technology.
2. By providing a variety of options, students will be able to choose the tool/activity they want to use versus all students needing to complete the same SEL activity. Allowing students to choose their own tools supports their individuality and the varying neurodiversity between them.
3. Some of the tactile items provided in this book (Section A) are associated with specific breathing and awareness activities. These activities support healthy habits and coping skills, especially when a student is feeling uncomfortable and anxious. Refer to the noted resource list for additional information on the research supporting these activities.
4. The SEL Tools are meant to be placed in students' own SEL Toolboxes and then stored in a specific area in the classroom for easy access. This area is referred to as the SEL Toolbox Area throughout this book and represents a self-regulatory space for children.
5. All the tools explained in this book support educational frameworks and standards. One framework is the SEL Framework. The educational standards include the National Health Education Standards (NHES), as well as many state-level standards/requirements. All these frameworks and standards support overall wellness for young people.
6. The overall concept of students having their own SEL Toolboxes in the classroom setting supports positive classroom management. After learning simple activities,

students can utilize their tools by setting a timer located in a self-regulatory area in the room. The teacher may choose to remind students about this opportunity, but the overall purpose is to help students master their own needs.
7. By allowing students choices due to their individual needs and wants, a positive classroom culture is supported. This culture is further enhanced by the creation of classroom expectations for all people in the room that allow for individual differences. Providing choices for SEL Tools supports this culture, which in turn, helps the teacher learn more about their students as individuals.

## Who This Book Is For

The *Tactile Tools for Social Emotional Learning* was written for **elementary school teachers** working with young people in the PreK to Grade 5 school setting.

The concepts found in this book can also be utilized in the following ways:

*For Children and Youth Programs:*
Many adults can teach children and youth healthy life skills to equip them with coping tools when challenges occur. This teaching supports resiliency in everyday situations as well as when more distressful events occur. Thankfully, many positive adults oversee programs and groups working with young people in which the tools and activities found in this book can also be utilized.

*By Families:*
Families can create a Family SEL Toolbox that is stored and used in a specific self-regulatory space in their household. After creating the actual "toolbox," each family member can create their favorite tools to be stored in the Family SEL Toolbox. Each member

of the family can also create their own personal Toolbox that is stored in their own space/room or in one general self-regulatory space in the household.

*In Social Workers' and Counselors' Offices:*
After creating an SEL Toolbox with some SEL Tools, the box can be placed either in a waiting area or the actual office of a social worker and/or counselor. If the Toolbox is placed in the waiting area, remember to provide written instructions for each tool placed in the box as well as the general purpose of the SEL Toolbox.

## Why This Book Was Written

Young people need to be provided with positive life skills to live their healthiest lives. Yet, if we weren't provided positive life skills earlier in our lives, how can we know what to do? That is why this book, *Tactile Tools for Social Emotional Learning*, was created.

Additionally, creating a positive culture with classroom management is an important yet challenging task. Figuring out how to do this can sometimes make us question why we choose to work in the educational field. Therefore, this book is to help you, the teacher, *create a positive culture and utilize a new classroom management technique.* This technique attempts to empower your students with self-regulation skills. Self-regulation includes having the skills to identify and manage feelings, especially when those feelings are uncomfortable or "yucky."

Another factor we need to consider is the loss of some healthy emotional coping skills during the COVID-19 pandemic. This loss of coping skills and how to express one's feelings is enhanced by the reality that some students are behind in their learning. When feeling frustrated, students may become more resistant to trying harder. Specific activities in this book seek to help students self-regulate themselves by "resetting their body systems"; this resetting includes guiding students who are feeling frustrated or unable to focus to go to their SEL Toolbox and choose an SEL Tool.

Last, *the Tactile Tools for Social Emotional Learning* and its corresponding activities support educational best practices and standards. Almost thirty (30) years ago, experts from a variety of fields noted the need for SEL among young people (Collaborative for Academic, Social, and Emotional Learning, 2022). These experts included people working in child development, education, emotional intelligence, bullying prevention, and other prevention and/or health education fields. The SEL framework was developed to focus on this need which includes a common understanding of what young people need for healthy development. Research tells us that young people who have utilized SEL in their education have an increased chance of a more positive mental and emotional wellness, improved academic outcomes, healthier relationships, and more! Administrators, teachers, and parents/guardians who support teaching SEL note the positive short-term and long-term benefits. For more information on this topic, refer to the next section on Educational Best Practices and Standards.

**Disclosure:** The SEL Tools and SEL Toolboxes are not intended to be used as a form of discipline. Instead, the information found in this book is solely for educational purposes. Please refer to qualified professionals, including your school's SEL professionals, medical doctors, and mental and emotional health experts, to support the wellness of the young people in your life as well as yourself.

## Educational Best Practices and Standards

### The SEL Framework: A Brief Overview
We are fortunate to live at a time in which students' educational success and wellness are recognized as needing more focus. If you grew up as I did, children were to be seen and not heard. Many young people who had behavioral or coping "issues" were sent to a resource room in school. Home life was not necessarily considered a factor in learning, and wellness referred to how a student's physical body was doing.

Over the past years, many people's voices are now being heard. We recognize the numerous factors impacting young people's overall wellness including social, emotional, environmental, mental, spiritual, and physical aspects.

As noted in the "Why?" section of this book, about thirty (30) years ago experts from a variety of fields noted the need for SEL by young people. These experts included people working in child development, education, emotional intelligence, bullying prevention, and other prevention and/or health education fields. The SEL framework (Collaborative for Academic, Social, and Emotional Learning, 2022) was developed to focus on this need which includes a common understanding of what young people need for healthy development.

Although time was needed for this framework to be better understood and supported throughout the world, many schools and families now embrace the need to focus on the "whole person," or the "whole child/student" depending on where you live. This "wholeness" refers to addressing a variety of wellness needs for young people to become intelligent and caring human beings.

So what is the SEL framework? This framework notes the need for young people to learn the knowledge, skills, and attitudes for developing five (5) concepts:

- self-awareness,
- self-management,
- social awareness,

- responsible decision-making, and
- positive relationship skills (Collaborative for Academic, Social, and Emotional Learning, 2022).

Some people may believe the above concepts are basic attributes all people should demonstrate from childhood. Sadly, not everyone learns these skills when they are younger. Some children are exposed to a variety of influences that negatively impact these skills. Due to these reasons, schools are teaching life skills, including SEL, to young people for students to have healthy relationships with themselves and others.

In addition to the above five (5) concepts, the SEL framework notes the importance of having: healthy classroom environments; positive school culture, practices, and policies; authentic partnerships with families and other caregivers; and aligning learning opportunities with communities (Collaborative for Academic, Social, and Emotional Learning, 2022). Although young people can become competent in all five (5) concepts, having positive external support systems further enables students to be the best they can be.

For more detailed information on SEL please refer to the Collaborative for Academic, Social, and Emotional Learning at: https://casel.org/fundamentals-of-sel/.

## National Health Educational Standards (NHES): A Brief Overview

Professional school teachers are trained in educational standards specifically aligned to their subject area. For school health education teachers, we have the National Health Educational Standards (NHES). Currently, two editions of these standards exist: the 2022 revised edition by the National Consensus for School Health Education and the 2024 revised edition by the Society of Health and Physical Educators. Both versions of these standards are based on the following life skills:

- practicing healthy and safe habits, also referred to as self-management skills,
- accessing valid and reliable resources,
- demonstrating effective interpersonal communication,

- analyzing influences,
- effective decision-making,
- effective planning and goal-setting, and
- advocating (National Consensus for School Health Education, 2022; Society of Health and Physical Educators, 2024).

Overall, what we (school health education teachers) have recognized is that the former paradigm of lecturing to young people on a variety of topics while using scare tactics *does not* change or support healthy behaviors. But what *does* support positive behaviors is skill development taught by introducing specific skills, modeling these skills, providing opportunities for students to practice these skills, and then providing feedback to help students strengthen their skill ability. While this skill development is going on, we infuse functional health knowledge which is basic information on a variety of health topics.

The NHES are referred to in this book because often PreK to 5th-grade Teachers are asked to teach health education. Although many standards and performance indicators exist for these grade levels, the activities in this book best align with NHES #7, Self-Management skills (practicing healthy and safe habits), supporting the teaching of Health Education in the elementary school setting.

*Note:* Both the SEL framework and the NHES support young people learning how to self-regulate their feelings and thoughts, as well as to seek support when needed.

## Creating a Positive Classroom Culture

Before students begin creating their SEL Toolboxes and SEL Tools, remember to plan for a positive classroom culture. This includes asking yourself some simple questions and creating expectations of students (and the use of the SEL Toolboxes/Tools).

### The Classroom Culture

Ask any experienced teacher what the most important thing that we can do to make sure our students are successful and happy at school and, most likely, they will answer *"Create a positive classroom culture."* This means the teacher needs to create an environment in which:

- children feel safe and connected
- expectations are known, accepted, and followed
- students and teachers are held accountable

This book, *Tactile Tools for Social Emotional Learning,* supports a positive classroom culture yet it is highly recommended that the above three aspects are planned for before students enter the classroom.

This section provides some pointers on how to plan for this. First, consider the following questions:

1. *How inviting is your classroom?*
   Our environments are important, including the ones we learn in. Therefore, make sure your classroom is structured in a manner that is child-friendly. Perhaps you can have a fun theme to decorate the room that children can relate to and have areas where students' photos and/or work can be displayed.
2. *How will you get to know your students?*
   The subjects we teach are important. Yet, research tells us that students' success increases when they feel connected to their teacher(s) and each other. To become familiar with your students, plan for "getting to know you" and "show and tell" activities during the first weeks of the school year.

3. *Are you modeling the behaviors you hope to see in your students?*

    We need to "walk the talk." Yes, we are adults, yet many young people do not have positive role models in their lives. Please be a positive role model for your students, including allowing yourself to express feelings that are healthfully self-regulated.

4. *What classroom expectations are most important to ensure all students feel valued and heard, as well as ensuring inappropriate behaviors are corrected?*

    When the word "expectations" is heard, some people think of rules – strict rules – and a lot of them. Yet our role is not to control children. Instead, we need to provide children the space to learn and make mistakes while being held accountable for the mistakes. Having classroom expectations helps children know what is expected of them and the possible consequences of inappropriate behaviors, and supports self-regulation skills. Consider referring to the sample class expectations noted in the next section.

5. *How do you handle inappropriate behaviors?*

    Children will make mistakes which include sometimes displaying hurtful and/or disrespectful behaviors. When inappropriate behaviors occur, make sure consistency and fairness are followed in any action taken. The students need to know what consequences to expect and that corrective measures will be enforced. Some teachers discuss with their students the possible consequences of inappropriate behaviors at the beginning of the school year to further support a positive classroom culture.

    Also, please remember that when inappropriate behaviors are corrected it is the behaviors that should be referred to and not the students themselves. In other words, saying "Lori, some of the words I heard you say may be hurtful," instead of "Lori, you were hurtful." Rephrasing our statements requires patience and practice, yet this self-regulatory habit is so helpful to children.

Creating a positive classroom culture takes patience and time. There is no one solution to handle all challenges, so be creative and honest with the students and yourself.

## Classroom Expectations

Creating a positive and effective environment in the classroom is imperative for students' learning. Again, achieving this takes time and patience. Although some of us were told, "Don't smile until the December holidays," which implies you need to be strict for months into the school year, effective teachers need to figure out the balance of displaying their hearts (kindness) yet holding students accountable.

One recommendation for creating this balance is setting up classroom expectations at the beginning of a school year. Setting expectations helps students of all ages know what is expected of them (and the teacher) in which both the students and teacher can create these expectations together. In addition, expectations should be discussed with students to ensure clarification of each statement.

The expectations explained in this section support the creation of a positive classroom environment and can be used for students of all ages. Having two (2) or three (3) classroom expectations works well with younger children, while older children could have more. In addition, expectations for using the SEL Toolboxes and the Toolbox Area are also provided.

Classroom expectations can include:

A. *This is a safe classroom.*

   Schools are supposed to be a safe place so this expectation may seem redundant. Yet, children and youth should be told you will attempt to always keep them safe, as well as what this "safe" classroom looks, sounds, and feels like. Therefore, discuss what a safe classroom is about. This can also be a reminder that "hands are for kind touches (not hitting)" and items that can hurt others (for example, weapons) are not allowed.

B. *You are enough.*

   Students need to be reminded that they are important and do not need to look or "be" a certain way or be compared to their siblings, peers, etc. "You are enough" means all students are worthy, lovable, and important.

C. *All feelings are okay.*

This statement reminds us that the feelings we feel happen for a reason. There are no "good" or "bad" feelings; actually, try to take those words out of your vocabulary when referring to SEL. This is recommended because these words create judgments on our feelings which can make us want to hide or suppress them. Feelings, the ones we enjoy and the ones that are considered "yucky," are real and happen for a reason.

D. *Mistaeks are okay.*

As shown in the misspelled word above, it is okay for students, and teachers, to make mistakes. This also implies that the classroom is a safe place to learn which means making a mistake sometimes. This statement also supports the growth mindset of learning from challenges instead of hiding from them.

E. *You have the right to ask for what you need.*

Many of us were told, "Children should be seen and not heard." This expectation supports the opposite idea in which children can ask for the things they need, including time in the SEL Toolbox Area.

Expectations for using the SEL Toolboxes and/or the Toolbox Area can include:

- The students need to ask the teachers when they need or want to utilize the Toolbox Area.
- The agreed-upon time will be followed unless additional time is requested. For example, the timer is set for five (5) minutes.
- The use of a tool is for individual activities unless they have been permitted to take a peer's assistance.
- They need to speak in low tones to not distract other students.
- If several students are requesting to use their SEL Toolboxes, a five-minute session for the whole class can be considered. During this time, students would select tools from their Toolboxes and complete the corresponding activity.

Additional reminders to consider:

- Upon classroom expectations being created and discussed with students, create signs displaying the expectations. Place these signs in visible areas of the classroom, like the front board.
- To ensure the classroom expectations are working, identify specific times during the school year to check in with students. Some suggested times for elementary school teachers to complete check-ins include:
  - a few days or a week after the class expectations were created;
  - a month into the school year;
  - after school breaks/vacations; these check-ins remind students of the expectations after being away from the physical classroom for a while; and
  - at other times when students need reminders about the classroom expectations.
- If students or the teacher believe that an expectation needs to be altered, discuss this with the class. Having these discussions with students models the positive social and emotional skills we hope our students use in their lives.
- Children and youth take chances. These chances sometimes include not following expectations. Taking chances allows young people to figure out boundaries and learn about consequences. So, please, hold your students accountable.
- The SEL Toolbox Area is not a disciplinary space to be used as punishment for any reason. Instead, students should be complimented on recognizing their need to become centered by completing a simple activity for a period of time to self-regulate their behaviors.

## Basic Terminology

This section includes terms used throughout this book, as well as other terms related to wellness. Simple definitions are provided for each term.

*Centering:*
Centering refers to a technique a person utilizes to focus attention on something in the present moment. Commonly used to lessen anxiety, centering can help slow down a person's breathing.

*Coping Skills:*
The word "cope" means to deal with something that is usually uncomfortable or difficult. Coping skills are healthy habits children can be taught when they are experiencing uncomfortable feelings.

*Fidget:*
The word "fidget" can be used as a verb or noun.
   When used as a noun, fidget refers to an object held in one's hand that can be manipulated, squished, played with, etc. The purpose behind allowing students to have fidgets at their disposal in school is to provide an outlet for students to do something with their hands as they learn.
   When used as a verb, fidget refers to a person's small movements, typically of their hands and/or feet. Sometimes people are thought to be feeling anxious or nervous when they fidget. Yet, some teachers have noted that children are able to focus more when they are provided with an opportunity to fidget with an object in the classroom setting.

*Mindful:*
Although there are a variety of definitions of this word, for this book the following definition will be used: *being in the present moment.*

To practice being in the present, simple acts can be performed allowing a student to simply *"be"* and note what is happening *in the moment.*

The more we practice being mindful, the easier this habit becomes in which we choose to be in the now, not in the past or the future.

*SEL Tools:*
SEL objects that are tactile and aligned with simple activities.

*SEL Toolbox:*
A toolbox is often referenced as a storage cabinet or container that holds many household tools like hammers, screwdrivers, and wrenches.

For this book, a Toolbox is a simple box decorated by a student to store the SEL Tools they created that align with different activities.

*Self-Regulation:*
Self-regulation includes having the skills to identify and manage feelings, especially when those feelings are uncomfortable.

*Self-Regulatory Space:*
A self-regulatory space is a safe space in which a student can practice self-regulatory activities, like those found in this book.

This place can be a designated area identified in a classroom, a "nook" or corner area of a house or apartment, or an actual room that is available. If none of these places are available, a safe space can be created by using a blanket or sheet placed over some chairs to create a "tent."

Other terms that can be used for this classroom area include SEL Toolbox Area (used throughout this book), Reflection Zone, Mindfulness Area, Solitude Spot, Peaceful Nook, Calming Corner, Quiet Corner, Break Corner, Peace Space, Chill Zone, Zen Den, and Tranquil Sanctuary.

Creating a self-regulatory space signifies to children and youth, as well as adults, that
- All of us need time to be by ourselves; alone time helps us remember who we are and process our feelings.
- It is okay to take some time for oneself; this concept is important for teachers, parents, and caregivers to model for children too.

*Stress:*
Stress is sometimes referred to negatively. Yet the reality is that stress is a part of life. Stress starts with the first breath we take and ends with our last breath.

A general definition of stress is *the demands placed upon an object*. When we identify ourselves as the object, *stress includes the social, mental, emotional, environmental, physical, and spiritual demands placed upon us.*

The activities in this book attempt to help students have a positive relationship with stress. Having the perspective that stress helps people grow and can be a motivational factor is a realistic and helpful way of looking at life. This thinking aligns with having a growth mindset.

Some stress-related terms with simple definitions include:
- *Eustress* – beneficial demands placed upon a person that helps them grow.
- *Distress* – demands placed upon a person that can be considered negative or hurtful; at times, people create their own distress by attempting to resolve too many demands ("I have to do it all" kind of thinking).
- *Duress* – overwhelming stress.

*Tools:*
A simple definition for a tool is *a device held in the hand and used to carry out a particular function.*

The tools referred to in this book are simple tactile objects to remind students to pause, take a breath, and/or complete simple activities. Most of these tools are associated with a tactile object a student can hold in their hands.

*Wellness:*
Wellness is the highest level of health a person can reach. This includes balancing all aspects of a person's health including the social, mental, emotional, environmental, physical, and spiritual parts.

*"Yucky":*
The term "yucky" is often understood by younger people. "Yucky" is an uncomfortable feeling that we do not like because we feel sad, angry, anxious, hurt, discomfort, or unmotivated. "Yucky" is a feeling of dislike that can make our noses and eyes squish, make our tongues stick out, and cause us to say "blech" or some inappropriate words out loud.

## Additional Resources

To learn more regarding the research behind teaching self-regulatory skills, including breathing techniques and centering activities to children and youth, refer to:

*Anxiety Canada:*
A group providing updated information about anxiety as well as resources for helping children and youth with anxiety. Found at https://www.anxietycanada.com

*The Association for Supervision and Curriculum Development (ASCD):*
A well-known organization supporting educators with updated and impactful pedagogy. Found at: https://www.ascd.org

*Breathe for Change*
A provider of training programs that empower teachers and administrators in building stronger school communities. Programs include mindfulness, SEL, and yoga teacher training. https://breatheforchange.com

*Calm*
An online site and app providing a variety of music and sounds that are backed by science. Found at: https://www.calm.com (after the information about Calm)

*Collaborative for Academic, Social, and Emotional Learning (CASEL)*
A leader in the SEL movement, CASEL recognizes the essential need for students to learn self-awareness, self-management, social awareness, responsible decision-making, and relationship skills. Found at https://casel.org

*Harvard Health Publishing of Harvard Medical School's article titled "Relaxation techniques: Breath control helps quell errant stress response"*
A simple summary is provided explaining the benefits of performing breathing exercises. Found at: https://www.health.harvard.edu/mind-and-mood/relaxation-techniques-breath-control-helps-quell-errant-stress-response

*Mayo Clinic's Healthy Lifestyle Site*
This website provides updated information on how to live healthfully, including the importance of managing stress, being mindful, and completing breathing exercises. Found at: https://www.mayoclinic.org/healthy-lifestyle

*Mindful and Mindful.org*
A "mindfulness community" working to share a variety of mindfulness information, courses, and trainings with the world. Found at: https://www.mindful.org/about-mindful/

National Education Association's pdf titled "Backgrounder: The importance of social emotional learning for all students across all grades"
An overview of SEL including Core SEL Competencies, outcomes aligning with the competencies, and impact evidence of SEL. Found at: https://files.eric.ed.gov/fulltext/ED581059.pdf

*PBS for Parents*
The Public Broadcasting Service (PBS) provides adults with background information on young people's self-awareness. Found at: https://www.pbs.org/parents/learn-grow/all-ages/emotions-self-awareness

## References

Collaborative for Academic, Social, and Emotional Learning. (2022). *Fundamentals of SEL*. CASEL. https://casel.org/fundamentals-of-sel/

National Consensus for School Health Education. (2022). *National Health Education Standards: Model Guidance for Curriculum and Instruction* (3rd Edition). https://www.schoolhealtheducation.org/

Society of Health and Physical Education. (2024). *New National Health Education Standards*. https://www.shapeamerica.org/standards/health/new-he-standards.aspx

# Getting Started

The overall concept behind the *Tactile Social Emotional Learning Tools* is to help students create tactile objects to be utilized when students recognize the need to self-regulate themselves, including when feeling uncomfortable. These tactile objects, referred to as SEL Tools, connect with simple activities students would complete for this self-regulation.

**Disclosure:** The information in this book does not replace seeking professional support. If you notice a student is projecting unhealthy feelings that seem to require additional support and/ or is having hurtful thoughts, please seek support from the SEL professionals in your school, medical professionals, and/or other emotional and mental health experts.

## Basic Recommendations

The following recommendations are based on the concept of having a designated area for students to complete these self-regulation activities.

After reading the Getting Started Section in *Tactile Tools for Social Emotional Learning*, the author recommends:

A. Creating a Self-Regulatory Space in your classroom
B. Helping students create their own Social Emotional Learning (SEL) Toolboxes
C. Helping students make initial SEL Tools
D. Introducing additional SEL Tools over time

## A. Creating a Self-Regulatory Space in your classroom

a) Designate an area in your classroom as a self-regulatory space. The term "SEL Toolbox Area" will be used throughout this book to refer to this space. Feel free to call this space something else aligning with your classroom culture. Other terms that can be used for this classroom area include Reflection Zone, Mindfulness Area, Solitude Spot, Peaceful Nook, Calming Corner, Quiet Corner, Break Corner, Peace Space, Chill Zone, Zen Den, and Tranquil Sanctuary.

This self-regulatory space would store students' SEL Toolboxes as well as be equipped with extra copies of "tools" (for example, scrap paper, blank "Thank You" notes, as well as extra created SEL Tools) in case students misplace their own.

b) A simple timer is recommended to be placed in the self-regulatory space and preset to a specific agreed-upon time. Setting the timer for five (5) minutes works with many students.

c) Discuss with students the purpose behind the self-regulatory space. This space's purpose includes recognizing that sometimes a student may need to have "space" or alone time to figure out how to cope; this created space supports this habit in your classroom.

d) Explain how the SEL Toolbox area would be used. For example, either the student or teacher would recognize the student needing to use an SEL tool in which the student would go to the designated self-regulatory space (SEL Toolbox Area), set the timer, and quietly utilize one chosen SEL Tool until the timer goes off. After the set time is completed, the tool is placed back into the student's SEL Toolbox and the student returns to their desk.

*Note:* If individual SEL Toolboxes cannot be used in the classroom, an overall class "Toolbox" can be created and stored in a self-regulatory space. Alter the provided steps for an overall class toolbox.

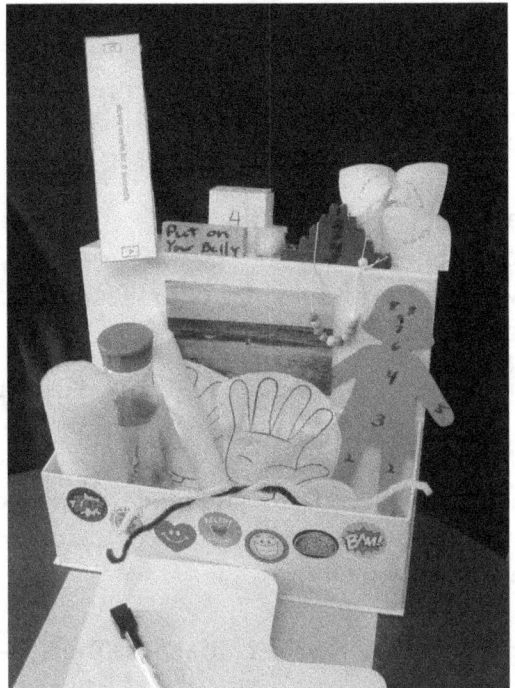

**FIGURE I.1** Example of an SEL Toolbox.

## B. Helping students create their own SEL Toolboxes

*Objective:* The purpose behind students making a toolbox is for each student to store their own SEL Tools that will be created during the following days or weeks. Allowing students to have their own toolbox supports the individuality of each young person as well as the sense of "ownership" of one's tools/toolbox.

*Materials needed:*
- ♦ Boxes or storage containers, one for each student; boxes can be empty shoe or tissue boxes; paper lunch bags can also be used; Note: Boxes will be referred to for the purpose of this book.
- ♦ Markers, stickers, paint, and/or other items students can use to decorate their SEL Toolboxes

**Steps for making the SEL Toolboxes (with students):**

1. Either supply boxes for students or request students to bring in small boxes to school to be used as SEL Toolboxes.
2. Ask students to decorate their SEL Toolboxes by:
    - attaching stickers to the box,
    - coloring/painting the box,
    - writing favorite sayings onto the box, and/or
    - gluing photos onto the box.

    Remind students to make sure their boxes represent who they are and do not display inappropriate decorations.
3. Explain that the created tools will be placed into each student's Toolbox after being made/provided.
4. If time allows, the first tool can be made and stored in each student's toolbox.

**C. Helping students make initial SEL Tools**

a) Choose the SEL Tools students will first create and learn about as well as how often a new SEL Tool will be introduced.

   Simple tools/activities to start with include:
   - Belly Breathing with a Hand (A1)
   - Breathing Out Bubbles (A2)
   - Clay (B2)
   - Favorite Photo or Drawing (B3)
   - Feeling Cards (C1)
   - "I feel" Statements (C5)
   - Yoga Cards (B5)

   How often a new SEL Tool is introduced is at the teacher's discretion. This can be weekly in which each Monday or Friday a new SEL Tool is presented.

b) After a tool is made, explain/model how each SEL Tool can be used with the aligned activity. Also, allow students time to practice the activity with the created tool.

c) Discuss with students how the SEL Tools can be utilized when a student identifies the need to practice a self-regulatory activity.

Remind students that when using the Toolbox Area a student would remove one SEL Tool from their SEL Toolbox and quietly complete the tool's corresponding activity for the set time. Also, remind students of what is expected of them when using the SEL Toolbox area.

D. **Introducing additional SEL Tools over time**

Continue to introduce additional SEL tools/activities throughout the school year. By introducing new SEL Tools, students will be reminded to continue to use their SEL Toolboxes.

## Other Times SEL Tools Can Be Used

The overall purpose of students making their own SEL Tools is to help students learn self-regulation skills. This means students are supported in listening to their feelings and bodies to then use an SEL tool as needed.

Also, everyone in the classroom can use an SEL Tool of their choosing at the same time when appropriate. For example: after lunch or Physical Education class, at the beginning or end of the day, and/or whenever the teacher (or a student) identifies the overall class needing some self-regulation time.

## How the SEL Tools and Activities Are Presented

The tools and activities provided in the *Tactile Social Emotional Learning Tools* book were developed by drawing on the author's thirty-plus (30+) years of classroom experience.

To best support your success, the SEL Tools and their corresponding activities are separated into three (3) overall sections:

### Section A: Tools for Breathing and Awareness Activities
All the tools in this area align with breathing and/or centering activities to help students lessen uncomfortable or anxious feelings and become more focused. All tools can be made with simple materials found at craft shops or online.

### Section B: Other Sensory Tools
A variety of tactile objects referring to students' senses are provided in this section. These tools and their corresponding activities refer to hearing, movement (for proprioception), smell, sight, taste, or touch. Many of the tools can be used in the SEL Toolbox Area or at students' desks.

### Section C: Tools Dealing with Words
The tools and their aligning activities provided in this section allow students to practice how to use words, including the writing and reading of them, as a coping tool. Beginning activities include students creating feeling cards and learning simple ways to express or identify their feelings. The intermediate and advanced activities are recommended for students who have basic writing and reading ability skills.

## How Each SEL Tool and Activity Is Organized

In each section, SEL Tools are organized by level of difficulty. These levels of difficulty were based on the author's educational and classroom experiences. For your students' success, *begin* with the most appropriate tools and activities that align with your students' abilities.

Each individual SEL Tool's information is organized into the following components:

*Activity Title:* A basic title referring to the SEL Tool and/or its corresponding activity.

*Level:* One (1) of three (3) activity levels are noted: Beginning, Intermediate, and Advanced. Please remember that activity levels can differ depending on each student's developmental stage as well as their basic understanding of self-regulation skills. The author recommends starting with "Beginning" activities. Also, due to some objects/tools requiring multiple steps for their creation, the teacher may decide to make them in advance.

*Tool for the SEL Toolbox:* The name of the SEL Tool to be placed into the created SEL Toolbox.

*Objective:* A basic explanation for why the tool and/or activity is recommended.

*Materials needed:* All materials needed to create the tool, including optional items. Sample activity sheets follow some tools/activities when appropriate.

*Steps for making and/or using the specific SEL Tool (with students):* Recommended steps for helping students make and/or utilize the tool.

*How each specific SEL Tool can be used:* Recommended ways in which students can use the tool either in the designated SEL Toolbox Area, at their desks, and/or at other times.

*Notes:* Specific considerations for some tools/activities are occasionally provided. Refer to these when appropriate.

**Remember:**

Students need to be reminded that when utilizing the SEL Toolbox Area, they would remove one SEL Tool from their toolboxes and engage in the corresponding activity for the set time. Reinforce the importance of remaining quiet and not distracting others in the classroom.

# A

# Tools for Breathing and Awareness Activities

## Tips for How to Use the SEL Tools in Section A

All SEL Tools in Section A align with the specific activities the teacher needs to teach students after the particular tools are made.

For these activities, explain to the students that they will be introduced to a variety of breathing and awareness activities, so they can decide which SEL Tool and activity they enjoy using the most. When doing this, allow students to share how they felt while completing the activities, reminding them that they might prefer certain activities over others.

*Please remind students that when utilizing the SEL Toolbox Area they should remove one (1) SEL Tool from their toolboxes and quietly engage in the corresponding activity for the set time.*

Notes:

- ♦ Completing different types of breathing activities may at first feel strange or uncomfortable for some students. If discomfort occurs, tell students to resume their natural breathing for the rest of the activity and pay attention to it.

♦ It is not recommended to force students to practice any breathing activities they do not like. Instead, a student can quietly sit or utilize another SEL Tool/activity while their peers continue with a specific activity.

**SEL Tools include:**

A1. Belly Breathing with a Hand (Beginning)
A2. Breathing Out Bubbles (Beginning)
A3. Listening Awareness (Beginning)
A4. Pinwheel Breathing (Beginning)
A5. Smile Breathing (Beginning)
A6. Sparkly Bottle Breathing (Beginning or Intermediate)
A7. Belly Breathing with a Block (Intermediate)
A8. Body Scanning (Intermediate)
A9. Box Breathing (Intermediate)
A10. Clouds as Our Thoughts Activity (Intermediate)
A11. Foot Awareness Activity (Intermediate)
A12. Lazy Figure 8 Breathing (Intermediate)
A13. Loving Kindness Activity (Intermediate)
A14. String of Beads Centering Activity (Intermediate)
A15. Triangle Breathing (Intermediate)
A16. Breathing as a Flying Bird (Advanced)
A17. Finding Our Center in 5 4 3 2 1 (Advanced)
A18. Loving Body Scan (Advanced)
A19. Moving a Paper clip on a Thread (Advanced)
A20. Parasympathetic "Reset" Breathing (Advanced)
A21. Progressive Muscle Relaxation Practice (Advanced)
A22. Slow Straw Breathing (Advanced)

## Activity A1: Belly Breathing with a Hand

*Level:* Beginning

*Tool for the SEL Toolbox:* Hand Cut-Outs (with Cotton Balls Inside)

*Objective:* This activity allows students to practice inhaling into their belly areas as their hands and the "hand templates" that are placed onto their bellies rise and fall. This type of breathing can help students feel calmer and more centered.

*Note:* Completing this type of breathing may feel strange or uncomfortable for some students at first. If discomfort occurs, tell students to resume their natural breathing for the activity.

*Materials needed:*
- copies of the provided hand template, one (1) per student,
- cotton balls to place in the created "hand," about three (3) for each student; putting cotton balls into the hand cut-outs creates a 3-D effect,
- white school glue,
- safety scissors,
- a comfortable place for each student to lie down to be able to see their belly areas rise and fall without straining their necks,
- small rugs or mats for students to lie on, one (1) per student; towels can also be used,
- a timer set to a specified amount of time for practice.

*Note:* If students are not able to use safety scissors on their own, cut out the hands from the templates before presenting this activity.

**Steps for making and using the Hand Cut-Outs (with students):**

1. Provide a copy of the "hands" template and a few cotton balls to each student.
2. Have each student cut out the two (2) paper hands, place the cotton balls in the center of their "hand," and then carefully glue the other "hand" around the cotton balls, along the outside section of the hands. The finished product should be a 3-D type of "hand."

3. Ask each student to lie down in a comfortable position and place their created "hand" on their belly areas. If available, students can lie on small rugs/mats. Students can also choose to prop a pillow or other soft article (ex. towel, sweatshirt) under their heads.
4. Before starting the breathing activity, have students close their eyes and take a few natural breaths to settle into this activity.
5. Ask students to open their eyes and look at the "hand" placed on their bellies. Tell students they can keep their "hand" cut-outs and/or their actual hands on their bellies to feel the inhalations and exhalations (belly rising and falling) for the activity. Then say:

    *We are going to now try to gently raise the "hand" on your belly a little bit by inhaling through our nose while raising our belly areas."*
6. Ask students to practice taking in a breath in which, while inhaling through the nose, the belly area is gently pushed up (out), raising the "hand."
7. Ask students to gently exhale through their mouths as their belly areas slowly go down, with their hands remaining on their bellies. Students should be able to feel their bellies slowly lowering.
8. Have students continue to breathe in and out of their belly areas with their hands gently rising for the inhalations and going down for the exhalations.
9. Have students resume their natural breathing for a few moments.
10. Allow students to discuss how they felt during this activity. Then have students place their Hand Cut-Outs into their SEL Toolboxes.

---

How the Hand Cut-Outs can be used as an SEL Tool:

Students can practice the Belly Breathing activity with their Hand Cut-out (or hand) on their bellies in the SEL Toolbox Area for a set time.

**Directions:**
1. Cut out each hand.
2. Glue cotton balls into the palm of one hand.
3. Place glue along the outline of one hand.
4. Glue the hands together.

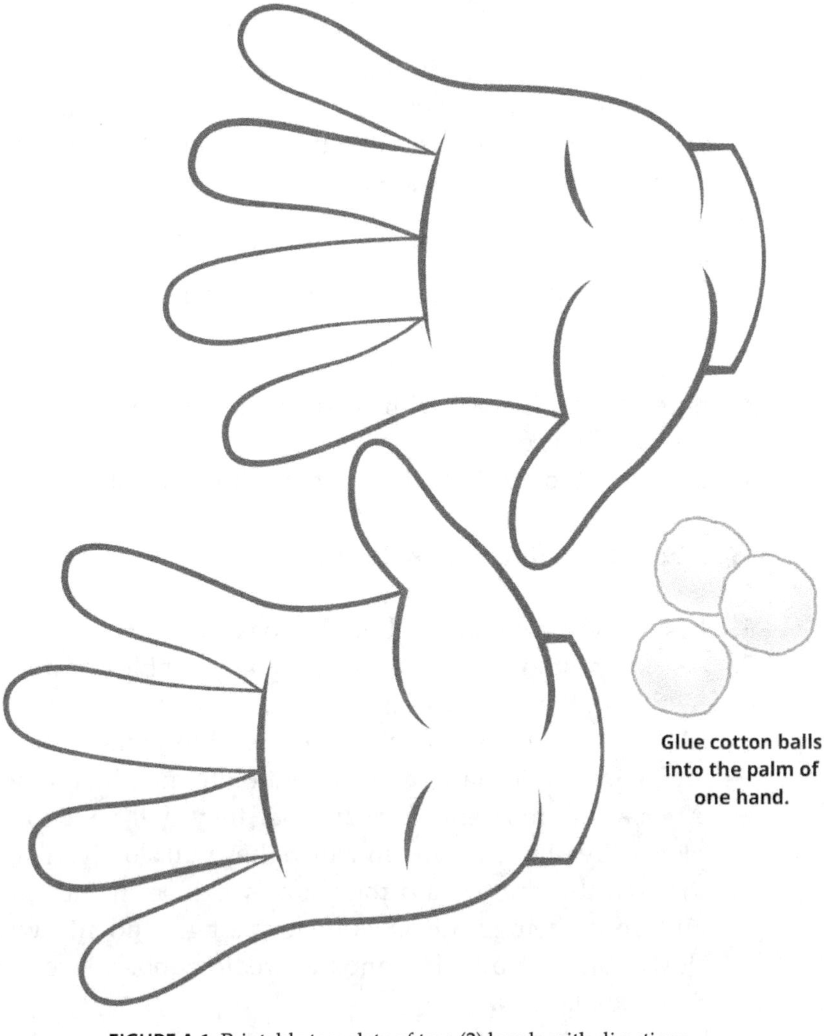

Glue cotton balls into the palm of one hand.

**FIGURE A.1** Printable template of two (2) hands with directions.

## Activity A2: Breathing Out Bubbles

*Level:* Beginning

*Tool for the SEL Toolbox:* A small container of Bubbles

*Objective:* Taking five (5) slow breaths, including long exhales, can slow us down and reset our breathing. This activity allows students to take these breaths while blowing bubbles, a simple activity many of us did as children.

*Materials needed:*
- small containers of bubbles, one (1) for each student; some craft stores sell these containers in their wedding sections,
- everyday dish soap with warm water (if needing additional mixture),
- a timer set to a specified amount of time for practice.

**Steps for using the Bubbles (with students):**

1. Distribute a container of bubbles to each student.
2. Ask each student to practice blowing bubbles on their own with the wands in their bubble container.
3. Make sure students are sitting in a comfortable position and ask them to start paying attention to their breathing. After a few moments, explain that they will next complete a breathing activity in which they will slowly inhale through their noses and then slowly exhale by blowing out from their mouths. Upon exhaling, students will slowly blow into their wands to create bubbles through their exhalations.
4. Say:
    *Stick the wands into the container to get some bubble mixture onto the end of the wand as you slowly inhale through your nose. Then slowly "blow"/exhale through your mouth to form bubbles into the air.*

5. Continue to lead this activity in which students are asked to inhale through their noses and then slowly exhale while blowing bubbles.
6. Allow students a few minutes to practice exhaling slowly, blowing bubbles, at least five (5) times.
7. Ask students to help clean up any bubble mixture from any areas, including the floor, if needed.
8. Allow students to discuss how they felt during this activity. Then have students place their Container of Bubbles into their SEL Toolboxes.

---

How the Container of Bubbles can be used as an SEL Tool:

Students can practice the Breathing with Bubbles activity with their bubbles in the SEL Toolbox Area for a set time.

Remind students to not distract their peers when choosing this tool from their Toolboxes and to clean up after themselves if needed.

## Activity A3: Listening Awareness

*Level:* Beginning

*Tool for the SEL Toolbox:* Template of a Young Person Listening or an Ear Stress Ball

*Objective:* One way of calming down is to shut one's eyes and simply listen. This activity allows students to do just that – close their eyes and listen to the variety of sounds in the room/area which may help them become more aware and calmer.

*Materials needed:*
- copies of the provided template printed on cardstock (young person pointing to their ears), one (1) per student, OR
- ear stress balls, one (1) per student, typically found in craft or novelty stores,
- a timer set to a specified amount of time for practice.

**Steps for using the Ear (with students):**

1. Distribute a copy of the provided template OR an ear stress ball to each student.
2. Discuss with students what the function of the ears is. One of the answers would be that ears allow us to hear a variety of sounds in our lives.
3. Explain that to hear things easier, this activity requires students to close their eyes, or close them a little bit, if they feel comfortable doing so.
4. Ask students to get comfortable in their seats and take a few slow breaths.
5. Have students close their eyes and listen. Allow students a minute to simply sit and listen. Remind students to pay attention to everything they hear.
6. After a minute, ask students to open their eyes and share what they heard. Often students will share a variety of sounds they often do not pay attention to or hear during school hours.

7. Have students close their eyes again to listen for some more time.
8. To conclude, ask students to share any new sounds they heard. Also, remind students that the provided diagram/ear stress ball serves as a reminder of this listening awareness activity.
9. Have students place their Listening Templates or Ear Stress Balls into their SEL Toolboxes.

---

How the Listening Template or Ear Stress Ball can be used as an SEL Tool:

Students can refer to their Listening Templates or Ear Stress Balls as a reminder to complete the Listening Awareness activity in the SEL Toolbox Area for the specified time.

The teacher can also display the Listening Template or an Ear Stress Ball to have the class complete this listening activity together.

**FIGURE A.3** Template example for the Listening Awareness activity.

Copyright material from Lori A. Reichel (2025), *Tactile Tools for Social Emotional Learning*, Routledge

## Activity A4: Pinwheel Breathing

*Level:* Beginning

*Tool for the SEL Toolbox:* Pinwheel

*Objective:* Taking a longer time to exhale than inhale "resets" the parasympathetic nervous system. Similar to the "Bubble Breathing" and "Parasympathetic Breathing" activities, this simple activity allows younger students to practice breathing with longer exhalations, helping them to feel calmer.

*Materials:*
- pinwheels bought online or at a dollar store, one (1) per student,
- a timer set to a specified amount of time for practice.

**Steps for using the Pinwheel (with students):**

1. Provide a pinwheel to each student. Allow students to play with the pinwheels for a few moments to figure out the best way they can make the wheels move/spin.
2. Explain to students that they will practice slow breathing in which their exhalations (breaths going out of their mouths) will provide the energy to spin their pinwheels.
3. Allow students to practice this breathing technique by explaining the following. Say:

   a) *Sit in an upright yet comfortable position while holding your pinwheel in front of you.*
   b) *Take a few natural breaths for yourself, noting how you are feeling.*
   c) *Slowly inhale through your nose.*
   d) *Then exhale out through your mouth, blowing slowly on your pinwheel, allowing your breath to make it spin.*
   e) *Slowly breathe in (inhale) again through your nose.*
   f) *Then slowly exhale out through your mouth, blowing on your pinwheel, allowing your breath to make it spin again.*

  g) *Continue breathing on your own, using your exhalation breaths to blow on the pinwheel for a few moments.*
  h) *Finish by resuming your natural breathing; note how you feel.*
4. Allow students to discuss how they felt during this activity and then ask them to place their Pinwheels into their SEL Toolboxes.

---

How the Pinwheel can be used as an SEL Tool:

Students can complete the Pinwheel Breathing activity in the SEL Toolbox Area for a set time.

---

## Activity A5: Smile Breathing

*Level:* Beginning

*Tool for the SEL Toolbox:* Smiley Sponge

*Objective:* The act of smiling releases hormones like dopamine, endorphins, and serotonin. The release of these hormones helps people feel better. This activity encourages students to smile while doing a breathing activity to experience this hormonal release.

*Materials needed:*
- sponges or stress balls with a smiley face, one (1) per student,
    OR
- large sponges cut into small circles (that would fit into students' hands) in which smiley faces are drawn, one (1) per student,
- a timer set to a specified amount of time for practice.

**Steps for using the Smiley Sponge (with students):**

1. Provide a smiley sponge to each student.
2. Explain to students that thinking of something positive can help people feel better and the act of smiling does that as well.
3. Ask students about past moments when they smiled or laughed a lot. Discuss how those times, and those smiles/laughs, helped them feel healthier and/or better.
4. Lead students into a breathing activity that incorporates smiling. Say:

    a) *Sit in an upright yet comfortable position while looking at your Smiley Sponge.* (Students may choose to hold their smiley sponges in their hands.)
    b) *Take a few natural breaths for yourself, noting how you are feeling.*

c) *Slowly inhale through your nose.*
   d) *Slowly exhale out and, as you do this, give a BIG smile.*
   e) *Slowly breathe in again, inhaling through your nose.*
   f) *Then slowly exhale making sure to give a BIG smile again.*
   g) *Continue breathing on your own making sure to have a BIG smile on your face as you exhale.*
   h) *Finish by resuming your natural breathing and noting how you feel.*
5. Allow students to discuss how they felt during this activity. Then have students place their Smiley Sponges into their SEL Toolboxes.

---

How the Smiley Sponge can be used as an SEL Tool:

Students can complete the Smiling Breathing activity by referring to their Smiley Sponges in the SEL Toolbox Area for a set time.

## Activity A6: Sparkly Bottle Breathing

*Level:* Beginning (if the teacher makes the Sparkly Bottle); Intermediate (if the students make the bottles)

*Tool for the SEL Toolbox*: Sparkly Bottle

*Objective:* Our parasympathetic nervous system sometimes gets disrupted or upset because of distress. This occurrence can negatively impact our daily lives, including sleep and digestion. Completing a simple breathing activity, like the one explained here, helps to calm this disruption. For this, shaking the Sparkly Bottle represents the disruption in the nervous system (after it is shaken), which can be calmed by the simple breathing activity provided here.

*Materials needed:*
- empty and clean eight-ounce (8) juice or water bottles with lids/tops (make sure the tops close tightly), one (1) per student,
- funnels that fit into the containers easily or pieces of sturdy paper rolled into funnels,
- water,
- at least two (2) floating items; examples include glitter, craft sand, and small plastic balls that fit into the bottles,
- a timer set to a specified amount of time for practice.

**Steps for making and using the Sparkly Bottle (with students):**

1. Distribute a clean bottle to each student.
2. Have students place the funnels at the top of their bottles and pour small amounts of the desired items into the bottles.
3. Ask the students to add clean water into the bottles leaving a little space at the top.
4. Have students close and secure the caps/lids onto the bottles, making sure no liquid leaks out if tipped to the side. If needed, use duct tape on the tops to avoid leaks.
5. Ask students to place their Sparkly Bottles in front of them.

6. Explain the following to students:
   *Imagine your Sparkly Bottle is your brain. Gently shake your bottle.*
7. Ask the students to shake the water bottles so they can see how the glitter/sand/objects inside move. Say:
   *The glitter and sand moving around in the bottles is similar to how our brains act when we experience certain feelings. The movement of the glitter and sand slowing down is similar to the activity in our brains as we calm down or become relaxed. We are now going to practice an activity that will help calm and settle our minds, just like the glitter and sand slowly settle down onto the bottom of the bottle once we stop shaking it.*
8. Continue the activity by saying the following instructions:

   a) *Sit comfortably in your chair, making sure your hands and feet are relaxed and not crossed. Take in a slow breath and notice how your body feels. Slowly exhale continuing to notice how your body slowly relaxes.*
   b) *Now shake your Sparkly Bottle before the next breath.* (Have students shake their bottles.)
   c) *Slowly inhale as you watch the glitter and sand move in the water. Then slowly exhale as you watch the glitter and sand slowly land at the bottom of the bottle.*
   d) *This simple activity of shaking the Sparkly Bottle and then taking slow inhales and exhales will help calm or settle our brains when we feel the need to calm down.*
   e) *Continue to slowly inhale and exhale as you use the Sparkly Bottle for the next few moments.*
9. Allow students to discuss how they felt during this activity. Then instruct the students to place their Sparkly Bottles into their SEL Toolboxes.

---

How the Sparkly Bottle can be used as an SEL Tool:

Students can shake their Sparkly Bottles and slowly inhale and exhale as they watch the objects in the bottle move and descend to the bottom while in the SEL Toolbox Area for a set time.

## Activity A7: Belly Breathing with a Block

*Level:* Intermediate

*Tool for the SEL Toolbox:* Wooden Block with "place on belly" written on it

*Objective:* If you ever observed a sleeping baby you would notice their belly rising and falling with each breath (belly breathing). As we grow older, we learn to expand our chest areas instead. This activity allows students to return to belly breathing while a block is placed onto their bellies and, with every breath, the block moves up and down. This type of breathing can help students feel calmer and more centered.

*Note:* This type of breathing may feel strange or uncomfortable to some students at first. If discomfort occurs, tell students to resume their natural breathing for the activity.

*Materials needed:*
- small wooden blocks, one (1) for each student,
- permanent markers/pens to write on the wooden blocks,

**FIGURE A.7** Example of a block.

- a comfortable place for each student to lie down to be able to see their belly areas rise and fall without straining their necks,
- small rugs or mats for students to lie on, one (1) per student; towels can also be used,
- a timer set to a specified amount of time for practice.

**Steps for making and using the Wooden Block (with students):**

1. Provide a block to each student. Have each student write "place on belly" on the wooden block with a permanent marker.
2. Ask each student to lie down in a comfortable position and place the wooden block onto their belly. If available, students can lie on small rugs/mats. They can also choose to use a pillow or any other soft article (ex. towel, sweatshirt) under their heads.
3. Begin this activity by asking the students to close their eyes and breathe naturally to settle into the activity.
4. Ask the students to open their eyes and look at the object placed on their bellies, without straining their necks. Students may also keep their eyes shut for this activity, in which case, they can sense their blocks going up and down as they breathe. Then say:

   *We are going to try to gently raise the wooden block a little bit by inhaling through our nose while raising our belly areas.*

   Ask students to practice taking a breath in which, while inhaling through the nose, the belly area is gently pushed up (out), raising the wooden block.

5. Ask students to gently exhale through their mouths as their belly area slowly goes down, with the wooden block remaining on their belly areas.
6. Ask the students to continue to breathe so their belly with the wooden block on top gently rises on the inhales and goes down on the exhales.

7. After the last belly breath is taken (the object went up and down for a last breath), ask the students to resume their natural breathing for a few moments.
8. Encourage the students to discuss how they felt during this activity. Then have students place their Wooden Blocks into their SEL Toolboxes.

---

How the Wooden Block can be used as an SEL Tool:

Students can practice the Belly Breathing activity with their wooden blocks on their bellies in the SEL Toolbox Area for a set time.

## Activity A8: Body Scanning

*Level:* Intermediate

*Tool for the SEL Toolbox:* Body Template with Numbers

*Objective:* Recognizing how our bodies are feeling is a recommended skill for emotional self-regulation. This activity allows students to slowly focus their minds on different body parts to notice the sensations/feelings of each part. The provided template serves as a visual for allowing students to focus on different body parts in a numbered manner.

*Materials needed:*
- copies of the provided template printed on cardstock paper OR premade body-figure cut-outs found at craft stores, one (1) per student,
- pens/pencils/markers if using a template without numbers,
- safety scissors to cut out the areas on the templates outside the body.

*Note:* After practicing this activity a few times as a class, most students can lead themselves through their own body scan in which the body template is a reminder of the order in which to proceed.

**Steps for making the Body Template if not using the provided template (with students):**

1. Distribute a body template to each student.
2. Ask students to number the parts of the body on the template in the following manner:

    1. = feet
    2. = lower legs
    3. = upper legs
    4. = belly area

       5. = chest area
       6. = the vertebrae (on the back)
       7. = shoulders
       8. = arms including the hands
       9. = the head
    3. Have each student cut out the area in the template which is outside the body with the safety scissors.
    4. Explain that the numbers on the body template represent the order in which the body scan activity will proceed. The scan will start with the feet, area #1, and eventually end with the head, area #9.

**Steps for using the Body Template with Numbers (with students):**

    1. Read the following steps while each student practices the body scan technique. Say:
       *Sit in a comfortable position. If you feel comfortable doing so, close your eyes.*
       *Notice your breathing as you slowly inhale and then exhale.*
       *Now bring attention to your feet to notice how they are feeling. Note any sensations you are feeling including if your feet are tingling, warm, cold, etc. Continue breathing as you pay attention to your feet.*
       *Next bring attention to your lower legs, noticing any sensations you are feeling.*
    2. Continue having students scan other body parts one part at a time. Parts include:
       - feet
       - lower legs
       - upper legs
       - belly area
       - chest area
       - vertebrae, going up the spine, one vertebra at a time
       - shoulders
       - arms including hands
       - the head

3. End the activity by asking students to slowly take a few natural breaths before opening their eyes.
4. Allow students to discuss how they felt during this activity. Then have students place their Body Templates with Numbers into their SEL Toolboxes.

---

How the Body Template with Numbers can be used as an SEL Tool:

Students can practice the body scanning activity by referring to their Body Templates with Numbers in the SEL Toolbox Area for the set time.

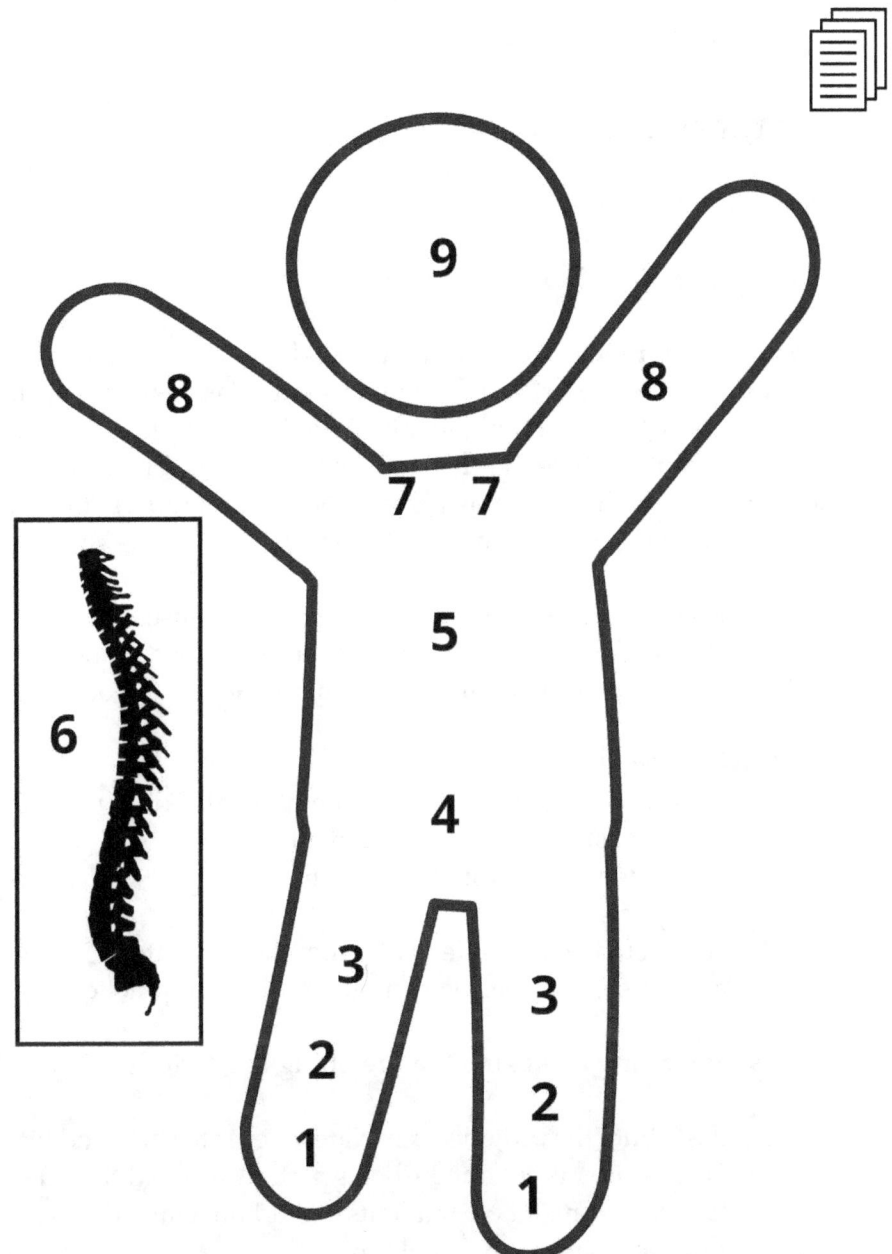

**FIGURE A.8** A printable template for the Body Scanning activity.

## Activity A9: Box Breathing

*Level:* Intermediate

*Tool for the SEL Toolbox*: Breathing Box

*Objective:* The practice of controlling one's breath helps our bodies slow down and "reset" our nervous systems. For this activity, an actual box is provided for students to hold onto while doing the counting of the inhale/hold/exhale/hold process. The purpose of this box breathing is to help students focus on different parts of a breath for the same amount of time.

*Fun Fact:* The Navy SEALS use this technique because it can help in highly stressful situations. Some athletes have also found that it helps control their breathing for swimming laps in a pool.

*Materials needed:*
- copies of the provided template of small boxes printed onto cardstock, one (1) per student,
- tape, a few pieces for each student,
- safety scissors,
- completed box sample made from the template,
- a timer set to a specified amount of time for practice.

**Steps for making and using the Breathing Box (with students):**

1. Distribute the provided template, one (1) to each student. Have students cut out the box's pattern and fold the sides to create a small box. Students should then tape the sides together to form an actual box.
2. Ask students to write "4" or "4 counts" on each side of the box. Make sure to demonstrate how to do this for students.
3. Explain that the box is going to be used for an activity called "box breathing." Say:

*This breathing includes inhaling for a count of four (4), holding the inhalation for the count of four (4), exhaling for the count of four (4), and then holding that exhalation for a count of four (4). Each part of the breath will be equal, like how the sides of a square are equal.*

4. To complete the activity, students can either:
   - Gently hold their boxes, slowly turning them while completing the activity. To focus on each part of the breath, students can also slide their fingers across the sides of the box for each step to help them complete each inhale, hold, exhale, and hold.
     OR
   - Simply look at their boxes to remind them to count to four (4) for inhaling, holding the inhalation, exhaling, and holding the exhalation.

5. To help students practice box breathing, say:
   a) *Get comfortable in your chair, closing your eyes if you choose to, yet holding the box.*
   b) *Take a few natural breaths, noting how your body feels while relaxing into your body's natural rhythm of breathing.*
   c) *Now we are going to begin box breathing. If you feel uncomfortable at any time, please return to your natural breathing.*
   d) *To start slowly inhale as you count: 1…2…3…4*
   e) *Hold this breath as you count: 1…2…3…4*
   f) *Slowly exhale as you count: 1…2…3…4*
   g) *Hold this exhale as you count: 1…2…3…4*
   h) *Slowly inhale again, as you count: 1…2…3…4*
   i) *Continue this breathing, noting the rhythm of four (4) counts to inhale, hold the inhale, exhale, and hold the exhale.*
   j) *As you are breathing in this manner, feel free to move the box in your hand to represent the next step or side of the box for breathing.*
   k) *Return to your natural breathing.*
   l) *Open your eyes.*

6. Allow students to discuss how they felt during this activity. Then have students place their Breathing Boxes into their SEL Toolboxes.

---

How the Breathing Box can be used as an SEL Tool:

Students can practice Boxed Breathing with their boxes in the SEL Toolbox Area for a set time.

## Directions:
- **Cut out the full diagram.**
- **Fold boxes at the seams to create a 3-D box.**

**FIGURE A.9** Printable template to make a 3-D box.

## Activity A10: Clouds as Our Thoughts Activity

*Level:* Intermediate

*Tool for the SEL Toolbox:* Cotton Balls on Cardstock

*Objective:* Performing breathing and awareness activities helps people focus on the present moment. While doing these activities, we often experience random thoughts that pop into our minds. This occurrence, sometimes referred to as "monkey mind," is okay, and practicing the act of identifying or noting the thoughts can help us return to the present moment and become more centered. This activity, "Clouds as Our Thoughts," provides students the opportunity to practice identifying their thoughts and then imagining their thoughts as clouds that "float away."

*Materials needed:*
- a handful of cotton balls for each student,
- pieces of cardstock, about four (4) inches by six (6) inches, one (1) per student,
- pens/pencils/markers/crayons,
- white school glue,
- a timer set to a specified amount of time for practice.

**Steps for making and using the Cotton Balls on Cardstock (with students):**

1. Provide a handful of cotton balls and a piece of cardstock to each student.
2. Ask students to write "my thoughts" on the cardstock and then glue the cotton balls around the words or onto different parts of one side of the cardstock.
3. Say:
   *Sometimes, when we practice breathing or other awareness activities, thoughts pop into our heads. This is okay – our brains are used to thinking a lot. To help our minds refocus on our breathing or other awareness, we will use this 'cloud card' to imagine our thoughts as clouds that float away.*

4. Ask students to sit in a comfortable position and complete the following centering activity. Say:

   a) *Sit comfortably on your chair and become aware of your breathing. You may close your eyes if you feel comfortable doing so.*
   b) *As you start noticing your breathing, choose one part of your breath to focus on. Perhaps you will choose your nose to feel the air going in and out of your nostrils, or your belly, or chest area as it rises and falls. Try to pick one part of your breathing and pay attention to it.*
   c) *Slowly continue to inhale and exhale paying attention to the chosen body part.*
   d) *As a thought pops into your head, distracting you from your breathing and the selected body part, imagine that thought as a cloud. Slowly, in your mind, imagine the cloud floating away. If it helps, touch the cotton balls on your cardstock to imagine the thought floating away like a cloud in the sky.*
   e) *After imagining the thought as a cloud that is floating away, return to focusing back on your breathing, to that chosen body part.*

5. Continue to have students practice breathing slowly for the allotted time.
6. Allow students to discuss how they felt during this activity. Then ask the students to place their Cotton Balls on Cardstock into their SEL Toolboxes.

---

How the Cotton Balls on Cardstock can be used as an SEL Tool:

Students can practice focusing on their breathing while noting their thoughts as clouds when sitting in the SEL Toolbox Area for a set time.

**FIGURE A.10** Example of cotton balls glued onto cardstock.

## Activity A11: Foot Awareness Activity

*Level:* Intermediate

*Tool for the SEL Toolbox:* Foot Outline with Steps

*Objective:* Upon completing research on reflexology, you would learn that we have many nerve endings in our feet. Touching areas of the feet, including giving gentle pressure to some spots, help some young people relax. This activity allows students to give themselves a gentle foot massage which may help them feel calmer and/or relaxed.

*Materials needed:*
- soap and water to clean hands (and feet if needed),
- outlines of a foot copied onto cardstock, one (1) for each student; a sample is provided,
- copies of "Steps for completing a foot rub" to be attached to the foot, one (1) per student,
- white school glue,
- a timer set to a specified amount of time for practice.

*Note:* Teach this activity with students sitting in a circle.

**Steps for making and using the Foot Outline (with students):**

1. Distribute a copy of the Foot Outline and a copy of the "Steps for completing a foot rub" to each student. Have students glue the printed steps onto their foot outlines. Students can also cut out the feet of their templates.
2. Have students wash their hands to prepare for the activity. Then have everyone sit on the floor in a circle.
3. Ask students to remove their shoes and socks and sit in a crossed-leg position, in which one foot rests on the other leg.
4. Refer to the following steps for students to give themselves a foot rub, pausing between each step to allow students to complete it. Say:

a) Begin by rubbing the bottom of your foot from the heel to the ball of your foot.
b) Then gently knead the different sections of the foot with your knuckles.
c) Gently squeeze the heel of your foot a few times.
d) Curl your toes and hold, then stretch out your toes and hold.
e) Hold out your foot, uncrossing the legs, and rotate the foot by making small circles with the foot in one direction, then rotate your foot in the other direction.
f) Cross your legs again placing the other foot on top. Perform the same actions with the other foot.

5. Allow students to discuss how they felt during this activity. Then have students place their Foot Outline templates into their SEL Toolboxes.
6. Ask the students to thoroughly wash their hands once again after they put on their shoes.

---

How the Foot Outline with the Steps can be used as an SEL Tool:

Students can practice the Foot Awareness activity in the SEL Toolbox Area for a set time. Remind the students to wash their hands before and after completing this activity.

# **Steps for completing a foot rub:**

1. Rub the bottom of your foot, from the heel to the ball, with your knuckles.
2. Gently knead the different sections of your foot.
3. Gently squeeze the heel of your foot a few times.
4. Curl your toes and hold, then stretch out your toes and hold.
5. Uncross your legs, hold out your foot, and rotate your foot by making small circles.
6. Rotate your foot in the other direction.
7. Repeat these steps for your other foot.

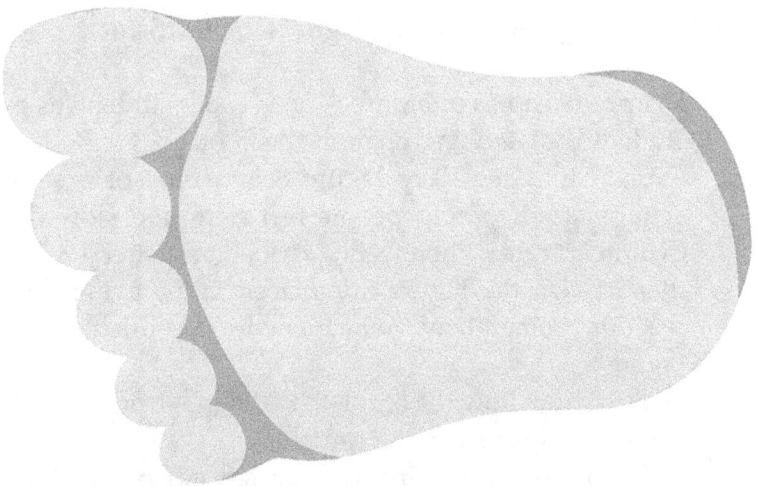

**FIGURE A.11** Printable template of a foot with simplified directions for completing a foot rub.

Copyright material from Lori A. Reichel (2025), *Tactile Tools for Social Emotional Learning*, Routledge

## Activity A12: Lazy Figure 8 Breathing

*Level:* Intermediate

*Tool for the SEL Toolbox:* Lazy Figure 8

*Objective:* The purpose behind the Lazy Figure 8 activity is to provide students with another way to pay attention to their breathing, including slowing down the speed of their breathing. Doing this helps students relax and feel calmer.

*Materials needed:*
- copies of the Figure 8 on cardstock paper, one (1) per student,
- a timer set to a specified amount of time for practice.

**Steps for making and using the Figure 8 on Cardstock:**

1. Distribute copies of Figure 8, one (1) per student, as each student is seated on a chair or the floor.
2. Explain that the Lazy Figure 8 is a type of breathing activity used to help people feel calm and slow down their heart rates when feeling rushed or distressed. To do this activity, the Figure 8 is placed in a "laying down" position, being "lazy," which is why it is titled the Lazy Figure 8.
3. Demonstrate how to complete the Figure 8 activity while using the Figure 8 on the cardstock.
   To do this, place a finger on the left side of the Figure 8 (as the Figure 8 is placed sideways) then demonstrate taking a slow breath, as your finger travels the Figure 8 for both the inhale and exhale.
4. To help students complete the activity, say:
   a) *Place your finger on the left side of the Figure 8.*
   b) *Slowly inhale as you trace your finger down then up along the Figure 8 to reach the other side.*

    c) *Slowly exhale as you trace your finger down then up, following the arrows, to reach the side we started with.*
    d) *Repeat this practice for a few more slow inhales and exhales.*
5. Allow students to practice this activity as they trace their fingers on the Figure 8 for five (5) complete breaths.
6. Allow students to discuss how they felt during this activity. Afterward, instruct the students to place their Figure 8s into their SEL Toolboxes.

---

How the Figure 8 can be used as an SEL Tool:

Students can practice the breathing activity with their Figure 8s in the SEL Toolbox Area for a set time.

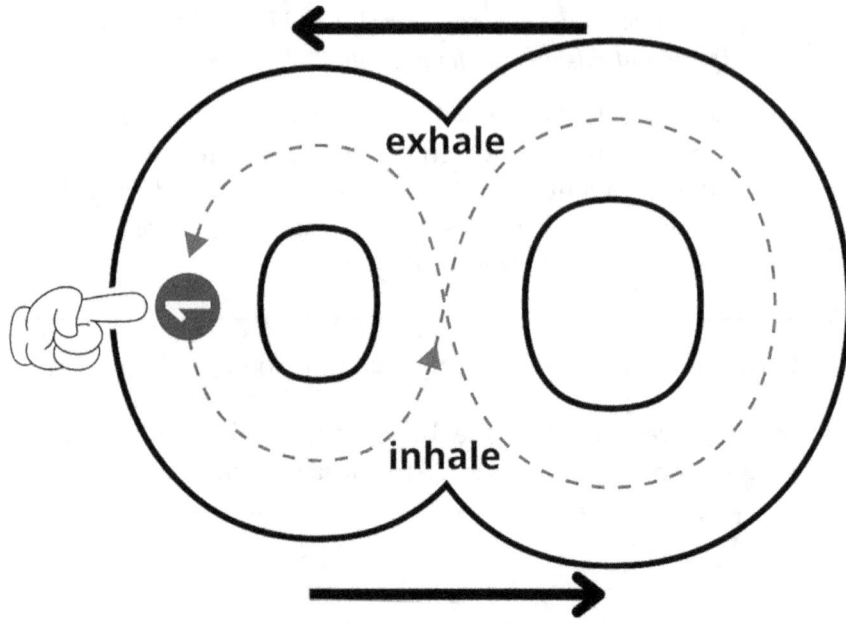

**FIGURE A.12** Printable template for practicing Lazy 8 breathing.

## Activity A13: Loving Kindness Activity

*Level:* Intermediate

*Tool for the SEL Toolbox:* Photo/Drawing of a Loved One

*Objective:* Thinking about the people and/or animals we love helps to release healthy hormones in our bodies which helps us feel better. This activity allows students to identify people/ animals they care about and then complete a centering activity while thinking about these people/animals.

*Materials needed:*
- a photo of a loved one (have students bring in a photo to place into their SEL Toolboxes before introducing this breathing activity),
  OR
- drawings created by students of people/pets they love,
- Optional: copies of the sentences found in Step 4d, one (1) per student,
- a timer set to a specified amount of time for practice.

**Steps for using the Photo/Drawing (with students):**

1. Ask students to take out the photo/drawing of a loved one.
2. Allow students to share who is in their photographs/ drawings, if they want to. Specific people and pets are possible answers.
3. Explain that this centering activity includes thinking positive thoughts about the person/pet in their photos/ drawings.
4. Lead students into the following activity. Say:
    a) *Sit in a comfortable seated position. If you feel comfortable doing so, close your eyes.*
    b) *Begin to notice your breathing as you slowly inhale and exhale.*

    c) *Now think about the person/pet in your photograph. For this, you can open your eyes and look at your photo/drawing.*
    d) *Imagine them being with you right now. And, as you picture them in your mind with you, say the following to them in your head:*
        *I hope you are happy.*
        *I hope you are safe.*
        *I hope you are healthy, peaceful, and strong.*
    e) *Continue thinking positive thoughts about this person/pet as you slowly breathe.*

5. Discuss with students about how they felt while performing this activity. Remind students that they can complete this activity about the person/pet, or anyone else, even when they are feeling angry toward the person/pet. Doing this can help lessen the angry feelings.
6. Allow students to discuss how they felt during this activity. Then have students place their photos/drawings into their SEL Toolboxes.

*Note:* Consider allowing the students to write the three (3) statements on the back of the photos/drawings.

---

How the Photo/Drawing of a Loved One can be used as an SEL Tool:

Students can look at their Photos/Drawings while saying the three (3) statements to their person/pet while in the SEL Toolbox Area for the set time.

---

## Activity A14: String of Beads Centering Activity

*Level:* Intermediate

*Tool for the SEL Toolbox:* String of Beads

*Objective:* Some students find counting while touching objects cathartic. This activity allows students to move beads along a string while completing simple inhalations and exhalations (breaths) for each strung bead. By completing this act students may feel calmer and/or centered.

*Materials needed:*
- sturdy string/rope/yarn with a diameter suitable to string beads; length can range from ten (10) to sixteen (16) inches depending upon each student's preference,
- ten (10) beads per student; make sure the beads are appropriate to the age of your students.

**Steps for making and using the String of Beads (with students):**

1. Provide a piece of string and ten (10) beads per student.
2. Have each student string their beads. Once all beads are strung, ask students to knot the ends of the string together. Help students make these knots if needed.
3. Explain and demonstrate the following breathing activity as students follow with their string of beads. Say:

   a) *Today we are going to practice counting breaths with our string of beads. To begin, make sure all beads on your string are pushed to one side of the knot.*

   b) *Now we are going to slowly take a breath, slowly inhaling then exhaling, as we move one of the beads to the other side of the knot.* (Model doing this.)

c) *Let's do this again, slowly taking a breath, inhaling then exhaling, as we move one of the beads to the other side of the knot.*
(Model doing this. There should be two (2) beads on one side of the string.)
d) *Now continue on your own, taking other slow breaths, one (1) per bead.*

4. Let the students continue to take slow breaths until all ten (10) beads have been moved to the opposite side of the knot.
5. End the activity by asking students to resume their natural breathing.
6. Allow students to discuss how they felt during this activity. Then have students place their Strings of Beads into their SEL Toolboxes.

---

How the String of Beads can be used as an SEL Tool:

In the SEL Toolbox Area with the set timer:

- Students can take ten (10) slow breaths while moving their beads, one at a time, to the opposite side.
- When feeling angry: Counting to ten (10) is a common coping strategy for diffusing anger. Students can use their String of Beads for this counting, slowly moving each bead one at a time.

Students can also fidget with the string of beads at their desks.

## Activity A15: Triangle Breathing

*Level:* Intermediate

*Tool for the SEL Toolbox:* Triangle made with cardstock

*Objective:* Similar to other breathing activities in this section, Triangle Breathing helps to "reset" the parasympathetic nervous system. This breathing activity helps students to relax, become centered, and/or lessen their feelings of anxiety.

*Materials needed:*
- copies of the triangle cut-outs on cardstock, one (1) per student,
- tape,
- safety scissors,
- a timer set to a specified amount of time for practice.

**Steps for making and using the Triangle (with students):**

1. Provide a copy of the triangle cut-outs on cardstock for each student. Ask students to cut out three (3) rectangles.
2. Have students tape the ends of each cut-out to one another, matching the letters at each end. A triangle should be formed.
3. Have students practice the Triangle Breathing activity. Say:

    a) *Sit in an upright yet comfortable position while holding the triangle.*
    b) *Take a few natural breaths becoming more aware of your feelings.*

c) *Put your finger on the letter "A" on the shortest side of your triangle. Slowly glide your finger over this small side as you inhale for the count of four (4) toward the letter "B."*
d) *Once your finger reaches the end, continue gliding it onto the next side of the triangle while holding your breath for the count of seven (7). Your finger will slide from the letter "B" to the letter "C."*
e) *Once your finger reaches the end, continue gliding it onto the next side of the triangle, slowly releasing your breath (exhaling) to the count of eight (8).*

4. Repeat this breathing by saying the steps C through E again for students.
5. Ask students to continue this breathing activity on their own for a few moments.
6. Allow students to discuss how they felt during this activity. Then have students place their Triangles into their SEL Toolboxes.

---

How the Triangle can be used as an SEL Tool:

Students can practice the Triangle Breathing Activity when choosing to use the SEL Toolbox Area with the set timer.

**Directions:**
1. Cut out the three rectangles.
2. Tape the matching edges together.

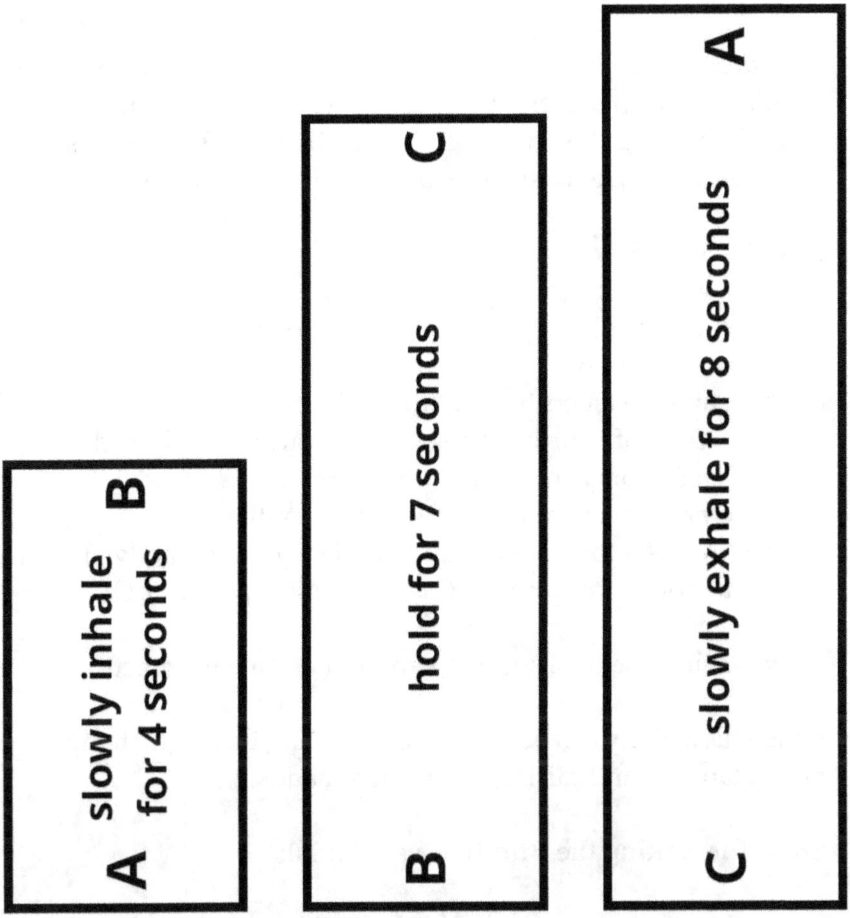

- Rectangle 1: A | slowly inhale for 4 seconds | B
- Rectangle 2: C | hold for 7 seconds | B
- Rectangle 3: A | slowly exhale for 8 seconds | C

FIGURE A.15 Printable template for making a tactile triangle.

Copyright material from Lori A. Reichel (2025), *Tactile Tools for Social Emotional Learning*, Routledge

## Activity A16: Breathing as a Flying Bird

*Level:* Advanced

*Tool for the SEL Toolbox:* The created "Bird"

*Objective:* Many children enjoy watching birds fly. This activity simulates birds flying slowly in which students inhale and exhale while imagining the wings of birds as they fly. The purpose of this activity is to help students breathe slower and relax.

*Materials needed:*
- copies of the provided template,
- crayons, colored pencils, and/or markers to color the "bird,"
- safety scissors,
- paper fasteners, two (2) for each "bird,"
- pieces of sturdy string about fourteen (14) inches in length for each "bird,"
- craft sticks to attach to the bottom of the "birds,"
- an object for creating holes in the wings and body of each template *(to be completed with adult supervision OR by an adult)*,
- a timer set to a specified amount of time for practice.

*Note:* This activity can be completed by using the "bird" template or by standing and raising one's arms/hands.

**Steps for making the Bird (with students):**

1. Print out the provided bird template, one (1) per student, and allow students to color in the template sections.
2. Ask students to cut out the bird's body and wings from the template, then carefully make holes into each part, as noted by the marked "hole" areas. For younger students, the teacher should make the holes in the templates.
3. Have each student push the two (2) paper fasteners into each large hole on the bird's body. Then ask students to attach one wing to each side of the bird by gently pushing

the fasteners into the holes on each wing. Students should then fold down the fasteners to secure the pieces together and make sure movement is possible for each wing.
4. Have students place the strings into the smaller holes found on the wings, knotting the strings loosely on the birds' backs, and allowing at least ten (10) inches to be left hanging (to move the wings). Help students who need assistance.
5. Ask students to glue craft sticks onto the backs of their birds leaving enough space to allow the holding of the craft sticks below the bird.

## Steps for completing the breathing activity while holding/looking at the Bird:

1. Ask each student to hold their bird in one hand and the strings for the bird in the other hand.
2. Begin the breathing activity by saying the following:
   a) *slowly breathe in as you gently pull the wings of your bird up;*
   b) *slowly breathe out as you release your hold of the string.*
3. Allow students to practice this a few times. Then continue the breathing activity using the "bird" as a reference and say:
   c) *Now put your birds to the side.*
   d) *Stand with your feet shoulder-width apart and arms down at your sides. If possible, stand facing your "bird" or something calming (you can allow students to look outside, if possible).*
   e) *Take two (2) to three (3) regular breaths.*
   f) *Slowly inhale and slowly raise your arms above your head.*
   g) *Slowly exhale as you bring your arms back down to the sides of your body.*
   h) *Continue inhaling, raising your arms above your head, and then exhaling, bringing your arms back down to the sides of your body.*
   i) *As you continue this breathing, imagine a bird slowly flying.*

4. After some time has passed, in which a few minutes of breathing has occurred, say:

   j) Place your hands on your hips in a superhero pose.
   k) *Take another two (2) to three (3) regular breaths.*

   *Note:* Research tells us that doing a "superhero" pose helps us to feel more in control, which is why the activity ends with students placing their hands on their hips.

5. Allow students to discuss how they felt during this activity. Then have students place their created Birds into their SEL Toolboxes.

---

How the Bird can be used as an SEL Tool:

Students can practice Breathing like a Flying the Bird activity with their created birds in the SEL Toolbox Area for a set time.

**FIGURE A.16** Printable template to make a movable paper bird.

Copyright material from Lori A. Reichel (2025), *Tactile Tools for Social Emotional Learning*, Routledge

## Activity A17: Finding Our Center in 5 4 3 2 1

*Level:* Advanced

*Tool for the SEL Toolbox:* Numbered Block Structure

*Objective:* Sometimes everyone can feel overwhelmed or anxious in which taking steps to ground or center us lessens these feelings. This activity helps students feel grounded/centered by using all five (5) of their senses in the 5 4 3 2 1 activity.

*Materials needed:*
- fifteen (15) small interlocking blocks per student (found at craft or dollar stores),
- permanent markers that can be used to write on the blocks,
    OR
- copies of the provided template, one (1) per student.

**Steps for making and using the Numbered Block Structure (with students):**

1. Distribute a set of blocks to each student.
2. Ask students to stack the blocks in this order:
    - five (5) blocks on the bottom
    - then four (4) blocks
    - then three (3) blocks
    - then two (2) blocks
    - and then one (1) block on top.

    Refer to the figure as an example of what the structure should look like.
3. Have students draw and/or write the following on each of the blocks:
    - The bottom level with five (5) blocks = an eye or the word "see."

- The fourth level = a finger/hand or the word "touch."
- The third level = an ear or the word "sound."
- The second level = a nose or the word "smell."
- Top/first level = a mouth or the word "taste."

4. Explain that each level of the blocks refers to one of the body senses in which each student will identify five (5) things they can see, four (4) things they feel/touch, three (3) things they can hear, two (2) things they can smell, and one thing they can taste, as they sit in their chairs.
5. Begin the activity below. Say:
   a) *Place your block structure on the desk in front of you to remind you of what we will be doing in this activity.*
   b) *Sit comfortably in your chair, taking a few breaths to note how your body is feeling.*
   c) *Now take three (3) slower breaths to figure out if doing this helps you feel calm(er).*
   d) *Next, look around the room and notice FIVE (5) things you see around you. Note these things in your mind and do not say them aloud. These things could be a pen, a spot on the ceiling, or anything in this room.* (Allow students a few moments to complete this.)
   e) *Now notice FOUR (4) things you can touch around you. Again, note these things in your mind. These things could be your chair, the ground under your feet, or the block structure you made.* (Allow students a few moments to complete this.)
   f) *Next notice THREE (3) things you hear. These things could be the humming of the projector, someone sneezing, or the rain outside. Focus on things you can hear outside of your body.* (Allow students a few moments to complete this.
   g) *Now notice TWO (2) things you can smell. These things could be the scent from your clothing, the air in our room, or the smells from a snack had earlier today.* (Allow students a few moments to complete this.)

      h) *Last, notice ONE thing you can taste. What does the inside of your mouth taste like – food from your breakfast or lunch?* (Allow students a few moments to complete this.)

      i) *Take a few slow natural breaths to finish this activity.*

6. Allow students to discuss how they felt completing this activity. Then have students place their Numbered Block Structures into their SEL Toolboxes.

---

How the Numbered Block Structure can be used as an SEL Tool:

Students can practice the 5 4 3 2 1 Centering Activity with the Numbered Block Structures in the SEL Toolbox Area for the set time.

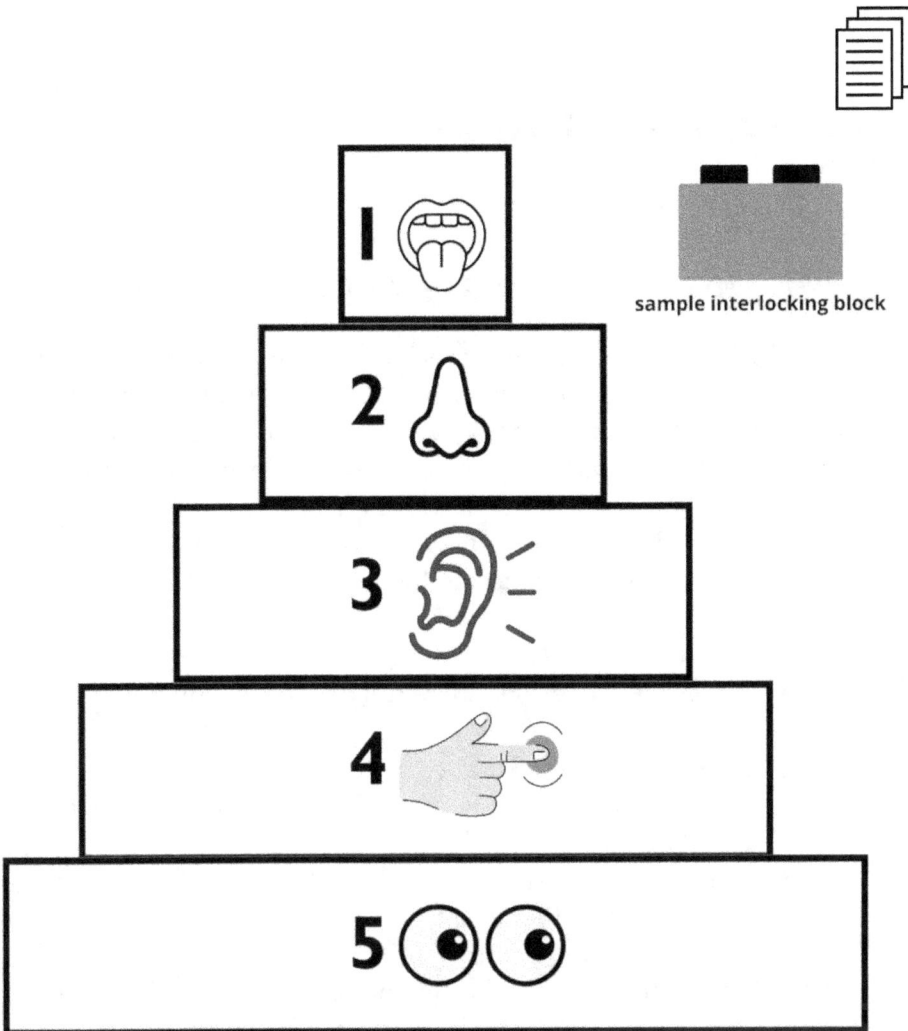

**FIGURE A.17** Optional template for completing the Finding Our Center in 5 4 3 2 1 activity.

## Activity A18: Loving Body Scan

*Level:* Advanced

*Tool for the SEL Toolbox:* Loving Body Template with Numbers

*Objective:* By the time children reach elementary school they have been bombarded with numerous media messages including those displaying certain body types. This exposure can initiate the focus on body parts students do not like instead of appreciating all of their body parts, as well as what their bodies can do. This activity, the Loving Body Scan, helps students appreciate their bodies while also centering them.

*Materials needed:*
- copies of the provided template printed on cardstock paper,
- pens/pencils/markers,
- safety scissors to remove the area outside the body on the template,
- script to read for the Loving Body Scan; simple steps are provided, yet other examples exist online.

*Note:* Students have physical differences. Therefore, before completing this activity, update how to phrase statements to ensure all students are supported during the activity.

**Steps for making and using the Loving Body Template (with students):**

1. Distribute a template to each student. Have students remove the areas outside the body of the template with a pair of safety scissors.
2. Have each student identify parts of their body that they like and/or appreciate by drawing a *heart* on the provided template. For example, if someone appreciates their eyes, they can draw a heart in the eye area.

3. Allow students to share where they drew their hearts if they want to.
4. Explain that the template will be used for an activity to help everyone think positively about their bodies. The numbers on the body template represent the order in which a Loving Body Scan will go in, starting at the feet, at area #1, and eventually ending at the head, at area #9.
5. Read the following steps for completing the Loving Body Scan. Say:

   a) *Sit in a comfortable seated position. Close your eyes if you feel comfortable doing so.*
   b) *Begin to notice your breathing as you slowly inhale and exhale.*
   c) *Now bring attention to your feet and say to yourself, inside your head, "thank you" to your feet for helping you walk, run, dance, and all of the other activities your feet help you to do. Continue your slow breathing as you silently say "thank you" to each foot.*
   d) *Next, bring attention to your legs, and say to yourself, inside your head, "Thank you" to your legs for activities your legs help you with. This includes helping you stand and sit, be active, giving you height, etc.*

6. Continue referring to the other body parts similarly, asking students to say "thank you" to the body parts while providing information on how these body parts help us. Examples of why we can be thankful for these parts include:

   ◆ belly area (a part we are often negative about, yet should be thankful for because it is our bellies that help digest food and keep us nourished)
   ◆ the chest area (which includes our hearts and lungs, helping our bodies transport nutrients and oxygen throughout our bodies)
   ◆ the vertebrae/the back (for helping us stand up straight especially during times we might feel weak)
   ◆ shoulders (for carrying the heavy loads we sometimes have to in our lives)

- hands and arms (to wave "hello" and to hug)
- the many parts of the head including our brains (for helping us to think, see, etc.)

Say: *Now, to end the activity, take another few slow breaths and then slowly open your eyes.*

7. Discuss with students how they felt when completing the activity. Then have students place their Loving Body Templates into their SEL Toolboxes.

---

How the Loving Body Template can be used as an SEL Tool:

Students can refer to their templates to practice the Loving Body Scan in the SEL Toolbox Area for a set time.

When working with students who are beginning puberty, the teacher can utilize this activity to support self-acceptance and self-love.

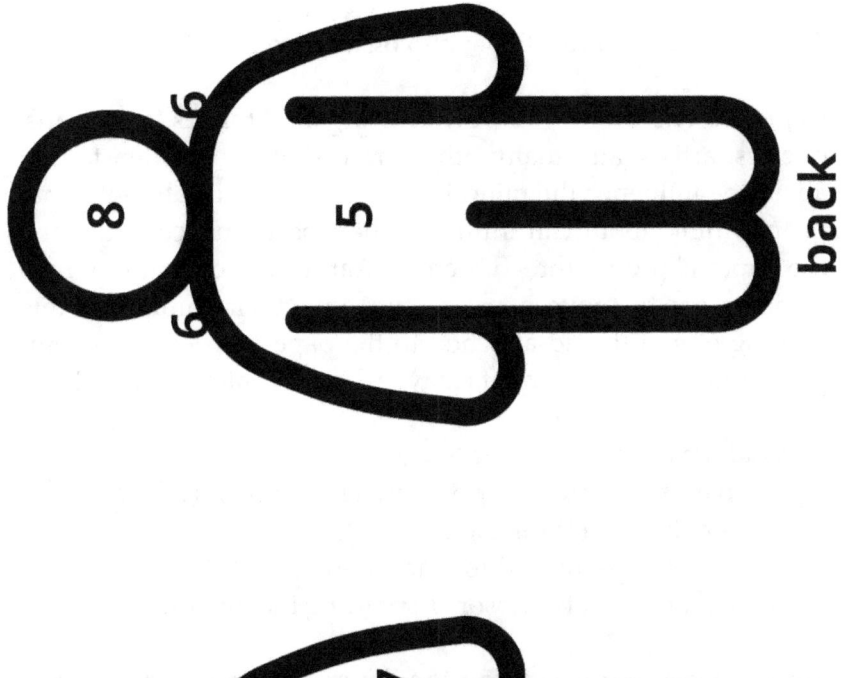
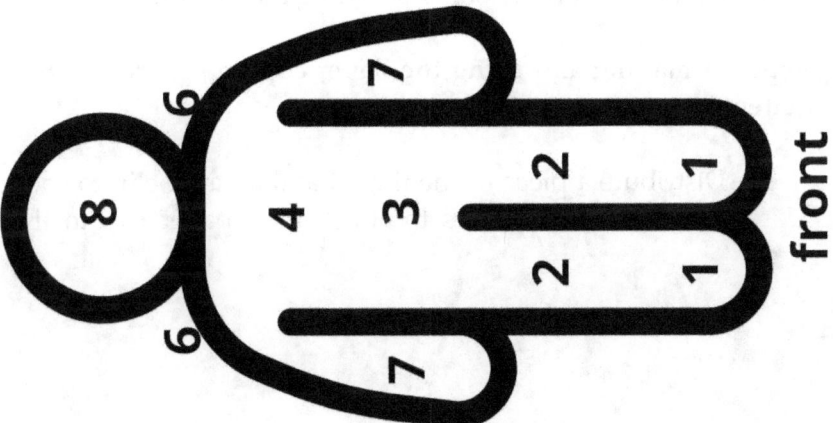

**FIGURE A.18** Printable template for completing the Loving Body Scan.

## Activity A19: Moving a Paper clip on a Thread

*Level:* Advanced

*Tool for the SEL Toolbox:* Paper clip on a Thread

*Objective:* The brain is a powerful organ. Athletes, musicians, doctors, artists, and many other professionals are often taught about the influence the mind has on the body. Simply put, what people think about can influence their performance. This tool, the paper clip on a thread, demonstrates this concept in which students try to move a paper clip with their thinking while holding onto a thread attached to the paper clip. And by completing this activity, students may feel more centered and calmer.

*Materials needed:*
- pieces of thread, approximately twenty (20) inches in length, one (1) for each student,
- paper clips, one (1) for each student,
- a pair of safety scissors for cutting the thread.

**Steps for making and using the Paper clip on a Thread (with students):**

1. Distribute a piece of the thread and a paper clip to each student. Ask students to attach their paper clip to the

**FIGURE A.19** Example of a paper clip attached to a thread.

thread by tying it onto the clip with a small knot. Assist those students needing help.
2. Explain that the brain is a powerful organ and, for this activity, students will be sending messages to the paper clip through the thoughts in their heads. This concept is often adopted by coaches of sports teams where athletes are taught about the influence the mind has on one's body (sports psychology).
3. Lead students into the following activity. Say:
   a) *Place your elbow on the table and hold the end of the thread in your thumb and index finger, making sure the paper clip hangs right above the table. (pause)*
   b) *In your mind, tell the paper clip to become still in which the paper clip simply hangs from the thread. (pause)*
   c) *Now tell the paper clip to swing on the thread from side to side. (pause)*
   d) *In your mind, tell the paper clip to become still again. (pause)*
   e) *Next, tell the paper clip to start moving in a circle. (pause)*
   f) *Then tell the paper clip to move in the opposite direction, in a circle. (pause)*
   g) *Rest your hand/arm.*
4. Lead a discussion about the activity by asking the following questions:
   - *How many of you had the paper clip slow down or stop when you told it to do so in your mind?* (pause to allow students to raise their hands)
   - *How many of you had the paper clip swing from side to side when you told it to do so in your mind?* (pause to allow students to raise their hands)
   - *How many of you had the paper clip move in a circle when you told it to do so in your mind? And then in the opposite direction?* (pause to allow students to raise their hands)
   - *Why do you think this happened?*

*Note:* Some students may not be able to move the paper clip at first. Yet, with practice, some movement often occurs.

5. Explain that people's thoughts can create movement due to messages sent through their nervous systems through the nerves. This is why athletes are often taught visualization skills, like creating images of how their bodies will move to throw a baseball or hit a tennis ball.
6. If time allows, have students form pairs. One student can watch their partner making the paper clip move, then have students switch.
7. Allow students to discuss how they felt during this activity. Then have students place their Paper clips strung on a Thread into their SEL Toolboxes.

---

How the Paper clip on a Thread can be used as an SEL Tool:

Students can practice trying to move their paper clips (by holding the threads) in the SEL Toolbox Area for a set time. Students can also practice taking slow breaths while doing this activity.

## Activity A20: Parasympathetic "Reset" Breathing

*Level:* Advanced

*Tool for the SEL Toolbox:* Breathing Protractor

*Objective:* Our parasympathetic nervous system sometimes gets disrupted due to distress which can increase our feelings of anxiety and negatively impact our work and sleep. Parasympathetic "reset" breathing helps to reset the system, helping us to feel calmer and more centered. The activity explained here provides students with the opportunity to try this breathing technique in which they complete three (3) to five (5) long exhalations after shorter inhalations.

*Materials needed:*
- plastic protractors, one (1) per student,
- permanent markers for writing on a protractor,
  OR
- copies of the provided "protractor," one (1) per student,
- a timer set to a specified amount of time for practice.

**Steps for making and using the Breathing Protractor (with students):**

1. Provide a protractor to each student.
2. Ask each student to write on the protractor in LARGE LETTERS the following:

    a) On the lower part, the straight-line noting inches from 0 to 8":
    
    *"Breathe in through your nose."*
    
    b) On the arc part of the protector (the curve) noting inches from 0 to 12":
    
    *"Breathe out through your mouth."*

    Make sure the ink is dry before starting the activity.

3. Have students practice the following breathing technique. Say:

   a) *Sit in an upright yet comfortable position while holding your Breathing Protractor.*
   b) *Take a few natural breaths for yourself, noting how you feel.*
   c) *Put one of your fingers on the edge of the protractor representing a "zero" (on the left corner), then slowly glide your finger over the straight part (inhale written section) then the curved part (exhale section), and back to where your finger started. As you are doing this, practice the following inhalations and exhalations.*
   d) *As your finger goes across the straight section of the Breathing Protractor slowly inhale through your nose.*
   e) *As your finger goes up and across the curved section of the Breathing Protractor slowly exhale out through your mouth*
   f) *Continue doing this breathing on your own for a few moments.*
   g) *Finish by resuming your natural breathing while noting how you feel.*

4. Let students discuss how they felt during this activity.
   - Then have students place their Breathing Protractors into their SEL Toolboxes.

---

How the Breathing Protractor can be used as an SEL Tool:

Students can practice the Parasympathetic Reset Breathing Activity using their Breathing Protractors in the SEL Toolbox Area for the set time.

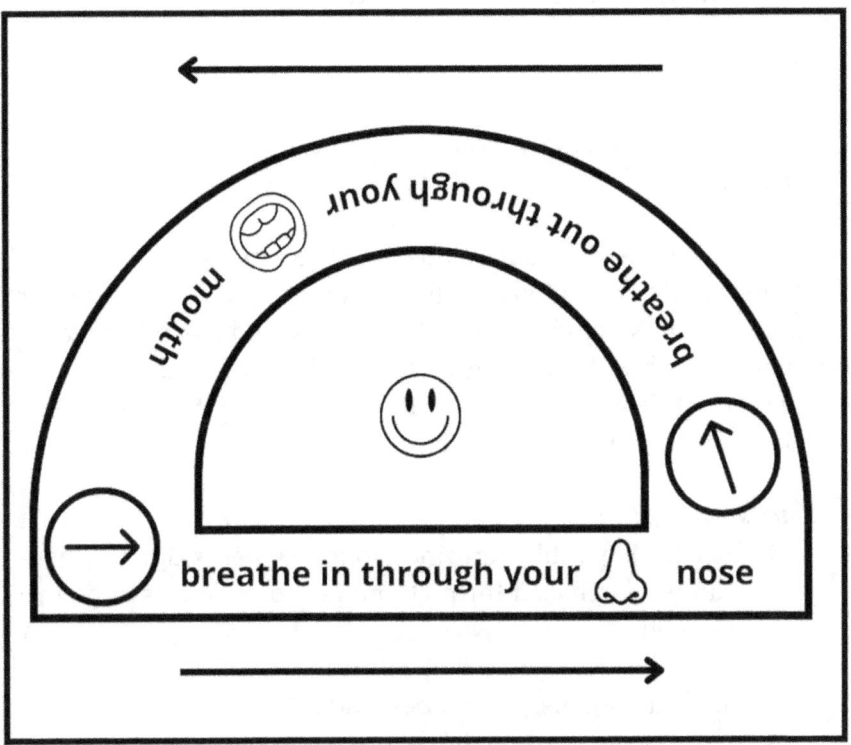

**FIGURE A.20** Printable template for completing the provided parasympathetic reset breathing activity.

## Activity A21: Progressive Muscle Relaxation Practice

*Level:* Advanced

*Tool for the SEL Toolbox:* Bendable Figurine or Stuffed Animal with numbers

*Objective:* Progressive muscle relaxation techniques help to relax different parts of the body, while also bringing awareness to our bodies. For this activity, students are provided steps to breathe in and out while tightening certain body parts, one at a time, and then relaxing them. Completing this activity typically helps students feel calmer and relaxed.

*Materials needed:*
- plastic bendable figurines, one (1) per student (these can be purchased through online stores or arts and craft outlets),
   OR
- stuffed animals, one (1) per student,
- permanent markers in different colors (or stickers with numbers on them),
- scripts for the actual activity; a simple script is provided. Other sample scripts/guides for progressive muscle relaxation techniques are found online (please make sure to use a reliable source).

**Steps for making and using the Bendable Figurine/Stuffed Animal (with students):**

1. Distribute a figurine or stuffed animal to each student.
2. Ask each student to write the numbers noted below onto the corresponding body parts by using a marker; if using the stickers, students are to place the appropriately numbered sticker onto the corresponding body part::

   1. = feet
   2. = lower legs

3. = upper legs
4. = belly area
5. = chest area
6. = the vertebrae (on the back)
7. = shoulders
8. = arms including the hands
9. = the face

If the bendable figurine/stuffed animal is too small, lessen the labeling to only the legs, the front belly area, the arms, the back, and the head.

3. Lead students in the following activity which includes tightening and relaxing body parts one at a time.
Remember to remind students to listen to their bodies; if any pain or cramping occurs, they should relax their bodies and not continue.
Say:

a) *Sit in an upright yet comfortable position. Place your numbered figurine/stuffed animal on the table before you.*
b) *Take a few natural breaths, noting how you are feeling.*
   *Feet:*
c) *Let's bring attention to our feet. Then slowly breathe in and tighten the muscles of your feet, yet not too hard to cause pain or cramping. Hold for three (3) to five (5) seconds.*
d) *Breathe out (exhale) and relax your feet. Notice how you feel.*
   *Lower legs:*
e) *Now let's bring attention to the lower legs. Slowly inhale while tightening the lower leg areas.*
f) *Breathe out (exhale) and relax your lower legs. Notice how you feel.*
   *Upper legs:*
g) *Now let's bring attention to the upper legs. Slowly inhale while tightening the upper leg areas.*
h) *Breathe out (exhale) and relax your upper legs. Notice how you feel.*

*Belly area:*
i) Now let's bring attention to the belly area. Slowly inhale while tightening the belly area.
j) Breathe out (exhale) and relax your belly area. Notice how you feel.

*Chest area:*
k) Now let's bring attention to the chest area. Slowly inhale while tightening the chest area.
l) Breathe out (exhale) and relax your chest area. Notice how you feel.

*Back:*
m) Now let's bring attention to the back. Slowly inhale while tightening the back areas.
n) Breathe out (exhale) and relax your back. Notice how you feel.

*Shoulders:*
o) Now let's bring attention to the shoulders. Slowly inhale while tightening the shoulders.
p) Breathe out (exhale) and relax your shoulders. Notice how you feel.

*Arms:*
q) Now let's bring attention to the arms. Slowly inhale while tightening the arms.
r) Breathe out (exhale) and relax your arms. Notice how you feel.

*Face:*
s) Now let's bring attention to the face. Slowly inhale while tightening your face, making a silly face.
t) Breathe out (exhale) and relax your face. Notice how you feel.
u) Now let's finish by resuming to our natural breathing, noting how we feel.

4. After students complete the activity discuss how they felt during and after it.

If any students experience aches or cramping seek out the school's nurse or another medical professional, if needed.

Also, consider allowing students to drink water; sometimes bringing attention to one's body in this manner increases a person's thirst.
5. Have students place their Bendable Figurines/Stuffed Animals with numbers into their SEL Toolboxes.

---

How the Bendable Figurine/Stuffed Animal with numbers can be used as an SEL Tool:

Students can practice the Progressive Muscle Relaxation activity by using their bendable figurines/stuffed animals as a guide in the SEL Toolbox Area for a set time.

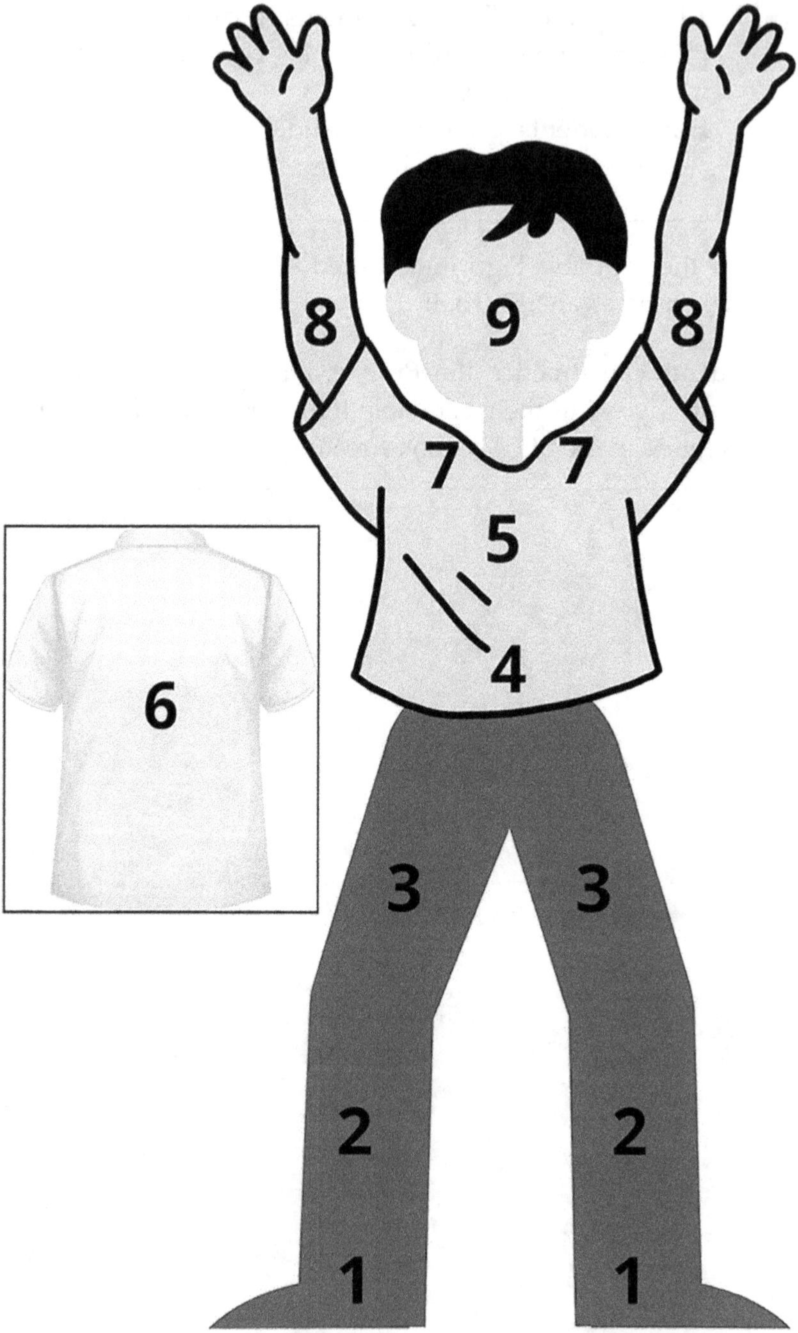

**FIGURE A.21** How a figurine would be numbered for the Progressive Muscle Relaxation activity.

Copyright material from Lori A. Reichel (2025), *Tactile Tools for Social Emotional Learning*, Routledge

## Activity A22: Slow Straw Breathing

*Level:* Advanced (due to students needing to recognize the Straw is to be used only for visual purposes)

*Tool for the SEL Toolbox:* A Straw

*Objective:* Taking long inhales and exhales through the mouth is another breathing technique to slow down heart rates and feel calmer. This activity allows students to practice this technique with a large straw being used as a visual reminder of breathing in and out through the mouth.

*Materials needed:*
- large straws (large openings), one (1) per student,
- a timer set to a specified amount of time for practice.

**Steps for using the Straw (with students):**

1. Provide a straw to each student.
2. Explain to students that the straw represents a breathing activity that includes inhaling and exhaling through the mouth only.
3. Lead students in the breathing activity. Say:
   a) *Sit in an upright yet comfortable position while looking at your straw.*
   b) *Take a few natural breaths, noting how you feel.*
   c) *Slowly inhale through your mouth as if you are slowly sipping some water through your straw.*
   d) *Pause for a moment.*
   e) *Slowly and smoothly exhale your breath through your mouth, as if blowing through the straw.*
   f) *Repeat this breathing activity three (3) times.*
   g) *Resume your natural breathing. Notice how you feel.*

*Note:* Remember to allow students to stop this activity if they experience discomfort.

4. Allow students to discuss how they felt during this activity. Then have students place their Straws into their SEL Toolboxes.

---

How the Straw can be used as an SEL Tool:

Students can complete the Slow Straw Breathing activity in the SEL Toolbox Area for a set time.

# B

# Other Sensory Tools

## Tips for How to Use the SEL Tools in Section B

Steps for a variety of tactile/sensory SEL Tools are provided in this section. Some of these tools have a specific activity associated with it while others do not.

For tools that have no activities associated with them, students can fidget/play with the created tool for a specified time. Some items can also remain at students' desks to be utilized as fidgets per teacher discretion.

*Please remind students that when utilizing the SEL Toolbox Area, they would remove one SEL Tool from their toolboxes and quietly engage in the activity corresponding to the tool for the specified time. This activity may be as simple as using the tool as a fidget.*

**SEL Tools include:**

- B1. Chenille Fidgets (Beginning/Intermediate)
- B2. Clay (Beginning)
- B3. Favorite Photo/Drawing (Beginning)
- B4. Sock Puppet (Beginning)
- B5. Yoga Cards (Beginning)
- B6. Favorite Scents (Intermediate)
- B7. Rain Stick (Intermediate)
- B8. Reminders of Nature (Intermediate)

B9. Slime (Intermediate)
B10. Soft Noodle (Intermediate)
B11. Stress Ball (Intermediate/Advanced)
B12. Decider Origami (Advanced)
B13. Labyrinth (Advanced)
B14. Laughter Tool (Advanced)

## Activity B1: Chenille Fidgets

*Level:* Beginning/Intermediate (depending upon the maturity level of students)

*Tool for the SEL Toolbox:* Chenille Fidgets

*Objective:* Often referred to as pipe cleaners, chenille stems are typically found in craft stores at reasonable prices. When provided to students, chenille stems can easily be used as a fidget for either a set time or at students' desks during the school day.

*Materials needed:*
- two to four (2 to 4) chenille stems per student,
- a timer set to a specific duration for students to play with the fidgets.

**Steps for using the Chenille Fidgets (with students):**

1. Distribute two to four (2 to 4) chenille stems per student. Students can choose stems of the same color or a variety of colors.
2. Allow students to play with the stems to either create a design and/or fidget with them for a few moments as a timer is set.

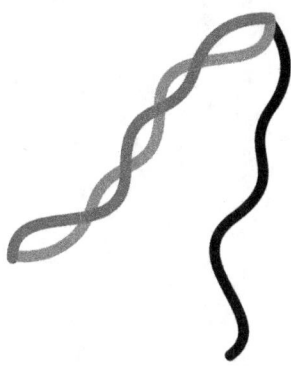

**FIGURE B.1** Example of a Chenille Fidget.

3. Have students place their Chenille Fidgets into their SEL Toolboxes.

---

How the Chenille Fidgets can be used as an SEL Tool:

♦ Students can fidget/play with the Chenille Fidgets in the SEL Toolbox Area for the specified time.
♦ The Chenille Fidgets can be kept at students' desks to be used anytime during the day (remind students of Classroom Expectations).

## Activity B2: Clay

*Level*: Beginning

*Tool for the SEL Toolbox:* Clay in a Storage Container/Bag

*Objective:* Many of us have experienced and enjoyed tactile play with clay. Often found in craft or hobby stores, clay can also be made with simple ingredients, as provided here. The purpose of having clay as a tool is to provide a safe object that is easily held in the hands for students to play or fidget with.

*Materials needed for each student's portion of clay as well as setting up clay-making stations:*

Option A:

- one (1) cup flour,
- one-half (½) cup salt,
- one-half (½) cup water (stir this into the mixture slowly),
- drops of food coloring.

Option B:

- one-half (½) cup cornstarch,
- one (1) cup baking soda,
- three-quarters (¾) cup water,
- drops of food coloring.

Option C:

- purchase ready-made clay, ensuring there is enough for each student.

Stations for making the clay:

- disposable or cloth table coverings on large tables for students to make the clay on,

OR
- large rags, pieces of cloth, or empty paper grocery bags to be placed onto students' desks, one (1) per student.

**Steps for making the Clay (with students):**

1. Decide beforehand where students will make the clay. As noted above, students can work at large tables or desks with the recommended table coverings.
2. Provide all ingredients to each student. Ask students to keep all items on the table coverings to limit clean-up.
3. Have students combine all ingredients and knead the mixture with their hands.
   *Note:* If the mixture is dry, students should add more water in small amounts.
   If the mixture is too sticky, students should add more flour/cornstarch in small amounts.
4. For colored clay, allow students to add drops of food coloring to their mixtures, four to six (4 to 6) drops at a time until the desired shades are reached.
5. Distribute the plastic bags or containers to have students store their clay, reminding them to make sure their bag/container is tightly closed. Have students place their clay into their SEL Toolboxes.

---

How the Clay can be used as an SEL Tool:

- Students can fidget/play with the clay in the SEL Toolbox Area for the specified time.
- The clay can be kept at students' desks to be used anytime during the day (remember to remind students of Classroom Expectations).

## Activity B3: Favorite Photo/Drawing

*Level*: Beginning

*Tool for the SEL Toolbox:* Favorite Photo/Drawing

*Objective:* Many of us enjoy being reminded of a special person, animal, place, or moment. Photos and drawings of these people, animals, places, and/or experiences can help us be reminded. The purpose of this tool is to allow students to simply refer to a photo or drawing of something they feel is special for a few moments. This simple act can help students feel calmer and more centered.

*Note:* Although this tool seems simple, many of the author's students have told her that seeing an actual photo or any other reminder of a special person, animal, place, or moment helps them to calm down when feeling distressed. The tactile-ness of taking out an actual photo/picture and taking time to look at it helps to release healthy calming hormones in the body.

*Materials needed:*
- ◆ appropriate photos of special people, animals, places, or special moments (students need to be asked to bring in an appropriate photo beforehand to place into their SEL Toolboxes),
    OR
- ◆ drawings created by students of people/animals/places/memories they enjoy.

**Steps for making the Favorite Photo/Drawing (with students):**

1. If allowing the use of photos: Ask students to bring in photos of special people and/or times.
   If students do not have access to photos: Ask students to think of a special person, animal, place, or experience and draw a picture of the person/animal/place/event to use as an SEL Tool.

2. Allow students to share with their peers what their photos/drawings are about to further impress upon the class how referring to this tool helps them remember special moments. This act of telling and hearing happy stories helps to release healthy hormones.
3. Have students place their photos/drawings into their SEL Toolboxes.

---

How the Favorite Photo/Drawing can be used as an SEL Tool:

In the SEL Toolbox Area with the set timer:

- ♦ Students can look at their Favorite Photos/Drawings.
- ♦ Students can draw other people, animals, places, or experiences on the blank paper in their SEL Toolboxes.

## Activity B4: Sock Puppet

*Level*: Beginning

*Tool for the SEL Toolbox:* Sock Puppet

*Objective:* Sock puppets have been created and played with by children for many years. Made with simple materials, playing with a sock puppet can help students pretend or practice having a conversation with another person. This pretending can also allow students to process feelings aloud and simply release uncomfortable feelings. All these actions support healthy social and emotional skills.

*Materials needed:*
- clean socks, one per student (can be bought from a thrift or bargain shop),
- markers for drawing on the socks,
- yarn (for sock "hair"),
- buttons or googly/wiggle eyes found at craft stores,
- other items that can be glued onto socks for sock puppets,
- fabric glue for attaching items onto socks,
- a timer set to your chosen amount of time for students to play with the sock puppets.

**FIGURE B.4** Example of a Sock Puppet.

**Steps for making and using the Sock Puppet (with students):**

1. Distribute one sock to each student.
2. Ask students to place one hand/arm into the sock, reaching their fingers to the foot part of the sock. Have students imagine how this foot area of the socks will become the heads of their sock puppets.
3. Allow students to design their sock puppets; their designs can include eyes, mouths, ears, and hair. If needed, students can work in pairs in which one partner places a sock onto their hand/arm while the other partner draws or glues onto the sock to ensure appropriate placement of parts.
4. Allow students time to play with their puppets, perhaps creating a puppet show with other students. Allowing students to do this will help students remember they can use their sock puppets for pretend, including pretending to speak with another person.
5. Have students place their Sock Puppets into their SEL Toolboxes.

---

How the Sock Puppet can be used as an SEL Tool:

- ♦ Students can quietly play with their created sock puppets in the SEL Toolbox Area for a set time. This play can be a pretend or practice for having conversation with another person.
- ♦ When conflicts occur within the classroom, the sock puppets can be used to help students talk with one another about the conflict. For this, the teacher or another student can help the students resolve their conflict.

## Activity B5: Yoga Cards

*Level*: Beginning

*Tool for the SEL Toolbox:* Yoga Cards

*Objective:* Slowly moving our bodies can help us clear our minds and feel more calm. Many young people agree with this, especially when they hold one "animal" yoga pose for a few moments followed by another "animal" yoga pose. This tool provides simple yoga poses on cardstock to allow students to perform simple yoga poses for a short time, transitioning from one pose to another.

*Materials needed:*
- copies of simple yoga poses onto cardstock (one sample is provided), one (1) set per student,
- safety scissors,
- a hole puncher,
- a paper clip or paper fastener for each student,
- a rug or mat in the designated SEL Toolbox Area to be used by students.

*Note:* Choose a variety of simple yoga poses to support the diversity and abilities of your students.

**Steps for making the Yoga Cards (with students):**

1. Distribute a copy of the yoga poses to each student.
2. Ask students to cut out each pose along the edges to create four (4) cards. If students cannot do this, the teacher may need to cut out the cards beforehand.
3. Have students punch a hole in the upper left corner of each of the cards and then pile/stack the cards, one on top of the other, pushing a paper clip or paper fastener into the holes.

4. After students have created their Yoga Cards, carefully demonstrate each pose displayed on the cards while allowing students to hold each pose for a few breaths/moments. Make sure students are completing poses in an open area in which students have their own spaces.
5. Have students place their Yoga Cards into their SEL Toolboxes.

---

How the Yoga Cards can be used as an SEL Tool:

Students can complete the yoga poses, holding each pose for a few breaths in the SEL Toolbox Area for the set time.

# Simple Yoga Poses

cow pose

cat pose

downward facing dog pose

child's pose

**FIGURE B.5** Yoga card examples.

## Activity B6: Favorite Scents

*Level*: Intermediate

*Tool for the SEL Toolbox:* Scented Object(s) in a Jar/Bag

*Objective:* Aromatherapy is the act of using certain scents for positive outcomes. A practice used for centuries, research has shown that the molecules from certain scented oils and objects travel from the olfactory nerves (nose nerves) to the emotional center of the brain, known as the amygdala, creating health benefits. Some students report experiencing relief from anxiety and depression when smelling certain scents, while others have found that using the olfactory nerves helps their thinking skills. Therefore, the purpose behind this scented object is to offer another sensory tool for students to refer to when feeling uncomfortable or unfocused.

*Materials needed:*
- items with safe natural scents; for example, cinnamon sticks, sprigs of rosemary, mint leaves, vanilla sticks, pine cones, safe essential oils,
- a large table with the above items spread out for students to explore/smell,
- cotton balls,
- sealable bags or jars.

*Note:* Remember to ensure students are not allergic to any of the chosen scents.

**Steps for making and using the Scented Object(s) (with students):**

1. Discuss what Aromatherapy is about with the students, including how smelling certain scents can help a student feel calmer, remember an event, focus on work, or have other positive reactions.

2. Refer to the variety of items placed on the table. After reviewing class expectations, allow students to explore the scents and choose one. For this exploration, ask students to hold the objects, slowly moving them back and forth a few inches away from their noses.
3. Once a student has chosen an object (for example, a pine cone) ask them to place the object into a sealable bag/jar. If a student chooses an essential oil, carefully apply a small drop of that oil onto a cotton ball for the student to place into their sealable bag/jar.
4. Demonstrate how to smell the scents by slowly moving the scented object under your nose and say:
 *To smell the chosen scent, we need to be careful to not put the object too close to our noses. Instead, we need to allow the scent to 'waft' in by slowly moving our object under our nose in a back-and-forth motion. Please make sure not to touch your nose or put the object too close to your nose.*
5. Have students demonstrate this smelling technique while ensuring each student is following the appropriate technique.
6. Have students place their bag/jar with their scents into their SEL Toolboxes.

---

How Favorite Scents can be used as an SEL Tool:

Students can sit quietly in the SEL Toolbox Area while occasionally smelling their scented objects for a set time.

## Activity B7: Rain Stick

*Level*: Intermediate

*Tool for the SEL Toolbox:* Rain Stick

*Objective:* Listening to rain can create calmer feelings for some people. For this tool, students create rain sticks to make the "sound" of rain as they slowly move their rain sticks. Completing this motion attempts to create a calming feeling for those who feel more centered when hearing the created sound and/or controlling the created sensation.

*Materials needed:*
- paper towel rolls, one (1) per student,
- colorful pens/pencils/crayons or stickers to decorate the paper towel roll,
- duct or wide masking tape, cut into three-inch (3") lengths, at least two (2) pieces per student,
- aluminum foil, about twelve-inch by twelve-inch ((12" x 12") sheets, one (1) per student,
- a mixture of small items including corn kernels, rice, and dried pasta placed into small paper cups, enough for all students,
- a funnel (a paper funnel can be used),
   OR
- clean and dry plastic water or juice bottles, one (1) per student (store-bought personal drinking bottles with bigger openings/mouths work well for Rain Sticks),
- colorful pens/pencils/crayons or stickers to decorate the paper towel roll,
- handfuls of colored straws, one handful per student,
- a variety of beans placed into small paper cups, about a quarter (1/4) cup per student,
- a quarter (1/4) cup of rice placed into small paper cups, one (1) per student.
- safety scissors

*Notes:* Make sure to check for student allergies before allowing students to obtain the items.

**Steps for making the Paper Towel Roll Rain Sticks (with students):**

1. Distribute a paper towel roll, two (2) pieces of duct tape, and a sheet of aluminum foil to each student.
2. Allow students to decorate their rolls by drawing, painting, and/or placing stickers.
3. Have students cover one end of the paper towel roll with tape, making sure the opening is fully covered.
4. Have students roll up their piece of aluminum foil and place the rolled foil into the paper towel roll.
5. Next, have students fill the inside of the paper towel roll with a mixture of the small items.
6. To finish the Rain Stick, have students cover the other end of the paper towel roll with tape, making sure the opening is fully covered.

**Steps for making the Bottle Rain Sticks (with students):**

1. Prep the bottles by first placing approximately a quarter (1/4) cup of beans (or more depending upon the size of the bottle) and a quarter (1/4) cup of rice into each bottle and placing the lids back onto the bottles.
2. Distribute the plastic bottles with the beans and rice to each student as well as a handful of straws per student.
3. Have students carefully cut their straws into a variety of lengths and then place all parts of the straws into their bottles.
4. Allow students to decorate their bottles by drawing, painting, or placing stickers.
5. Finally, have students cover their bottles with the lids, making sure the lids are tight.

*Note:* Both above Rain Sticks can have additional items added to them depending upon the size of the bottle and the sounds being created.

**Steps for using the Rain Sticks (with students):**

1. Allow students a few minutes to play with their created Rain Sticks. This would include students recognizing the sounds made when their sticks are moved in a variety of ways, including side-to-side and up-to-down.
2. Ask students to hold their Rain Sticks so they are vertical and no sounds are made. Say:
   *Before you move the Rain Sticks again, please carefully listen to my instructions. When I say 'Okey-dokey,' I want you to slowly move your Rain Sticks; as you slowly move them, the objects from the bottom slowly move to the other side and a sound much like "rainfall" is heard. Try to control the speed of the objects by how you move your Rain Sticks.*
3. Allow students to slowly move their Rain Sticks, listening to the sounds. Then discuss with the class what was it they heard and how they felt as they attempted to control the speed of the objects inside as they moved from one end to the other.
4. Explain that the created sound mimics the sound of rain and, depending on how quickly the Rain Stick is moved, the sound of the rain will range from gentle to hard.
5. Have students practice this slow movement again for a few moments.
6. Have students place their Rain Sticks into their SEL Toolboxes.

---

How the Rain Stick can be used as an SEL Tool:

In the SEL Toolbox Area, students can slowly move their Rain Sticks for a set time to control the speed of the objects as they move from one side of the stick to the other.

   *Note:* Remind students not to distract other students when using their Rain Stick.

## Activity B8: Reminders of Nature

*Level*: Intermediate

*Tool for the SEL Toolbox:* Reminders of Nature in a Container/Bag

*Objective:* Research tells us that being with nature supports health benefits including lowering heart rates and cortisol levels, as well as calming minds. The purpose behind this tool, Reminders of Nature, is to allow students to reflect on nature and how they feel when they are in a natural, outdoor setting.

*Materials needed:*
- access to a natural outdoor setting,
- outdoor items that can be found in our living environments (examples include pine cones, beach sand),
- storage containers or bags for these items,
- additional class supervisors to ensure the safety of all students.

*Note:* Make sure to check for student allergies before allowing students to procure these items. Also, ensure only safe plants are found in the natural setting. For example, make sure there is no poison ivy or poison oak in the area.

**Steps for making and using the Reminders of Nature (with students):**

1. Schedule a class adventure in which students are allowed to go into a natural outdoor setting. This setting may be a nearby park, arboretum, or beach area. Make sure to have the appropriate number of supervisors present to ensure the safety of students.
2. Discuss with students how being outside in a natural environment has been shown to help people feel calmer and happier. Perhaps allow students a few moments to pause and then identify how they feel in that setting.

3. Ask students to find two (2) or three (3) natural objects that they enjoy looking at and/or feeling. Objects might be a leaf, a pebble, or some sand. Remind students to choose safe and healthy objects and to refer to an adult when unsure.
4. Have students place their natural objects into their storage containers/bags to place into their SEL Toolboxes. Make sure that certain objects, like rocks, are cleaned before being stored.
5. Optional: Allow students to share the objects they found with their classmates. As they share what their objects (tools) are, encourage further discussion on the importance of spending time in natural environments.

How the Reminders of Nature can be used as an SEL Tool:

Students can refer to the natural objects in their storage containers/bags in the SEL Toolbox Area for a set time. Students can also recall a favorite memory regarding why they like their reminders of nature.

## Activity B9: Slime

*Level*: Intermediate (due to the slime being made by the teacher)

*Tool for the SEL Toolbox:* Slime in a Container

*Objective:* Just like some young people like to fidget with clay, slime is another favorite item to manipulate in one's hands. The objective behind using slime as a tool is to provide students with another tactile and stretchable object to fidget or play with for some time.

*Materials needed for each student's portion of slime:*
- one (1) cup (an 8-ounce bottle) of white school glue,
- food coloring (different colors can be provided),
- one-and-a-half to two (1 ½–2) tablespoons of contact saline solution or slime activator solution found at craft stores or online,
- one (1) tablespoon baking soda,
- small plastic bags or containers with lids, one (1) per student.

*Note:* The following steps are for the teacher to make slime for the whole class and then introduce the tool to students. If allowed, students can also make the slime.

**Steps for making the Slime (by the teacher):**

1. Add glue and food coloring into a bowl and stir until combined.
2. Mix in baking soda and stir.
3. Slowly mix in the saline solution or slime activator adding half of a teaspoon at a time. If the mixture is too sticky/slimy, add more saline solution.
4. Knead the slime with your hands. It will feel wet and gooey at first, yet kneading it for a short time allows the ingredients to blend and become slime.
5. Make sure to wash your hands after making the slime.

**Steps for using the Slime (with students):**

1. Explain to students that everyone will receive some of the slime and they are allowed to play or fidget with it for a few moments.
2. Distribute slime to students.
3. After a few moments of play, distribute the plastic bags/containers and have students store their slime, reminding them to make sure their bags/containers are tightly closed.
4. Have students place the slime into their SEL Toolboxes.

---

How the Slime can be used as an SEL Tool:

- ♦ Students can fidget/play with the slime in the SEL Toolbox Area for the specified time.
- ♦ The slime can be kept at students' desks to be used anytime during the day (remind students of Classroom Expectations).

## Activity B10: Soft Noodle

*Level*: Intermediate

*Tool for the SEL Toolbox:* Soft Noodle

*Objective:* Noodle floats, found in many discount stores, have a variety of uses for teachers. For this SEL tool, noodle floats would be cut into specific lengths and used in a variety of ways, as noted below, which support a variety of emotional coping skills.

*Note:* Remind students not to distract others when using their Soft Noodles.

*Materials needed:*
- noodle floats found in dollar stores, cut into lengths of about six (6) inches; one (1) per student

How the Soft Noodle can be used as an SEL Tool:

When stored in students' SEL Toolboxes:

- Students can squeeze their Soft Noodles during a specific time or, if allowed to be kept at students' desks, utilize them throughout the school day.
- If allowed and using a timer for a short period, students can gently tap objects in the SEL Toolbox Area to create soft drum-like sounds with the Soft Noodles.
- A small object can be placed into the center of the noodle and students can attempt to control the speed of the object traveling from one opening of the noodle to the other. If using the Soft Noodle in this manner, the length of the noodle can be longer.
- Tapping has become more popular over the past years in which the phrase Emotional Freedom Technique (EFT) has been used frequently in the elementary school setting. If students are allowed to use the Soft Noodle as a tapping tool, please research this technique to provide safe steps for all students.

Other ideas:

- If a variety of sizes/lengths of noodles are provided, students can use the noodle pieces as blocks.
- If numbers and letters are written onto small pieces of noodles, students can create words or math problems with the noodles.

## Activity B11: Stress Ball

*Level*: Intermediate (if the teacher makes the Sparkle Bottle); Advanced (if the students make the bottle)

*Tool for the SEL Toolbox:* Stress Ball

*Objective:* Many store-bought stress balls are used in classrooms. Typically, students are allowed to keep these balls at their desks to squeeze/fidget with throughout the day to help them self-regulate and/or concentrate. For this SEL Tool, stress balls are made by students to be used in the same manner and then stored in the SEL Toolboxes.

*Materials needed:*
- small non-latex balloons, approximately two (2) for each student (additional balloons can be used to create a colored design),
- rice or small birdseed,
- small cups or measuring cups,
- funnels; these can be created with papers that are rolled and then taped,
- large containers to catch rice/seeds when stress balls are being created.

*Note:* Ask students to work in small groups to create their stress balls. The making of these stress balls requires patience and time, as well as some cleaning afterward. Although the classroom area may get a little messy, students typically enjoy creating their own stress balls.

**Steps for making and using the Stress Ball (by the teacher only or with students):**

1. Distribute one (1) balloon per student. Ask students to blow air into their balloons a few times allowing the balloons to stretch.

2. Have students place the bottom of a funnel into the opening of their balloons.
3. Have students slowly scoop the rice/seeds into small cups then pour the rice/seeds into the funnels.
4. After a few scoops of rice/seeds have been funneled into the balloon, ask students to squeeze the balloons, moving the rice/seeds to the sides and bottoms of the balloons.
5. Continue to have students add more scoops of rice/seeds into their balloons until the filled balloons fit into their palms. Students can then tie the opening of the balloons into knots to keep the rice/seeds in the balloons.
6. Be available to help students who cannot tie their balloons.
7. Provide an additional balloon of a different color to each student. Have students cut the opening of the balloon off, then cut out other small sections of the deflated balloons. Students can then slide the cut balloons over their stress balls to create simple designs.
8. Allow students to practice squeezing their Stress Balls, explaining that sometimes squeezing something helps a person feel better.
9. Have students place their created Stress Balls into their SEL Toolboxes.

---

How the Stress Ball can be used as an SEL Tool:

♦ Students can squeeze their Stress Balls in the SEL Toolbox Area for the specified time.
♦ The Stress Balls can be kept at students' desks and used anytime during the school day.

## Activity B12: Decider Origami

*Level*: Advanced

*Tool for the SEL Toolbox:* Decider Origami

*Objective:* Many of us may remember making an origami decision-making tool when we were younger. The purpose of this tool was to make simple decisions. For this SEL Tool, the Decider Origami will help students decide how to cope when experiencing uncomfortable feelings. Another purpose behind this activity is to teach the hands-on craft of making origami which can be used as a healthy coping skill.

*Materials needed:*
- papers cut into squares, one (1) piece per student; if using regular paper, cut the paper into eight-and-a-half inch squares (8.5 x 8.5),
- sample Deciders for students to refer to.

**Steps for making the Decider Origami (with students):**

*Note:* As the steps are explained model each step to create a sample Decider. Also, have the sample Deciders placed throughout the classroom for students to refer to.

1. Provide a piece of paper to each student. Explain that the next SEL Tool includes making a form of origami.
2. Ask students to complete the following steps for making creases in their papers by saying:

   a) *Place your paper on the table and fold one top corner to the opposite bottom corner, making a right angle with the paper. Press down onto the folded paper and then open the paper back to its original square shape.*

   b) *Fold the other top corner to the other bottom corner, making another right angle. Press down onto the folded paper again, then open the paper back again to its original square shape.*

3. With the paper fully opened, follow the steps below to create the inside sections (for writing numbers and coping tools). Say:

   a) *Fold one top corner to the center of the square while also folding the opposite corner to the center of the square in which both corners almost touch one another. If done correctly, the paper will look like a hexagon with the longer sides having two equal lengths.*
   b) *Fold the other top corner to the center of the square while also folding the opposite corner to the center in which both corners almost touch one another. If done correctly, the paper will now form a smaller square (smaller than its original size) in which creases will form eight (8) small triangles.*
   c) *Flip the square over in which a square with no folded corners is in front of you and repeat steps a and b. At this point, there should be eight (8) triangles: two (2) in each of the four (4) larger triangles.*
   d) *In each smaller triangle write eight (8) numbers, one per section.*
   e) *Open up the folded triangles. Think of four (4) healthy coping tools you like to use and write them on the underside of the numbered sections. Options might include playing with clay, belly breathing, reading your letter to yourself, etc.*
   f) *Refold the triangles, displaying the smaller square with the numbers written on the small triangles.*

4. For the outside sections (for writing colors), say:

   a) *Turn the Decider over in which four (4) smaller squares appear to make a square.*
   b) *Write four (4) different colors on the top sections/triangles.*

5. For the final folds, say:

   a) *Turn the Decider over again to display your numbers.*
   b) *With the smaller squares in front of you (showing the numbers), fold the top of the square, the top section with four numbers, onto the bottom. Doing this just created a crease for using our Decider.*

c) *Unfold to display the smaller square and hold the right side of the square onto the left side, making another rectangle. Again, we just created another crease to use our Decider.*

6. To use the Decider, say:

   a) *Once constructed, there should be four (4) outside tabs noting four (4) different colors. Inside will be eight (8) numbers and, beneath these numbers, a variety of coping tools will be written.*
   
   b) *To make sure the Decider was made correctly, ensure the inside that displays the numbers is facing you. Place your thumbs into the two lower spaces between the paper. Place one or two fingers from both hands into the two higher spaces between the paper.*
   
   c) *As the thumbs/gingers are inserted into these sections, gently press them together. The Decider will most likely start to shape up in which the squares noting your chosen colors will appear on the top section.*

7. Allow students to play with their created Deciders, moving sections with their fingers.

## Steps for using the Decider:

1. Have students work with a partner to use their Deciders.
2. As the Decider faces the partner (the student making the decision), the partner should first choose one of the presented colors. The owner of the Decider then opens and closes the Decider for each letter of the chosen color. For example, if the color red is chosen, the Decider is opened/closed three times, one time for the letter "r," a second time for the letter "e" and a third time for the letter "d," showing inside sections.
3. Once the Decider is opened, four (4) numbers will appear on the inside sections. One of these numbers should then be chosen by the partner in which the Decider is opened and closed the corresponding number of times of the chosen number. For example, if number three (3) is chosen, the Decider is opened/closed three (3) times.

4. For the last decision, the partner is to pick another number from the inside sections that show four (4) numbers. The chosen numbered section is then lifted by the student to reveal the coping tool for the partner to use for a few minutes.
5. Allow students to switch places with their partners to make decisions with their partners' Deciders.
6. Have students place their Deciders into their SEL Toolboxes.

---

How the Decider can be used as an SEL Tool:

In the SEL Toolbox Area with the set timer:

- Students can play with the Deciders or make new ones (making origami is another coping skill for some students to relax or become centered).
- Students can use the Deciders (or have peers help them use the Deciders) to choose another SEL tool to use.

Also, the teacher's Decider might be used when everyone in the class wants to use the same SEL Tool for a set time.

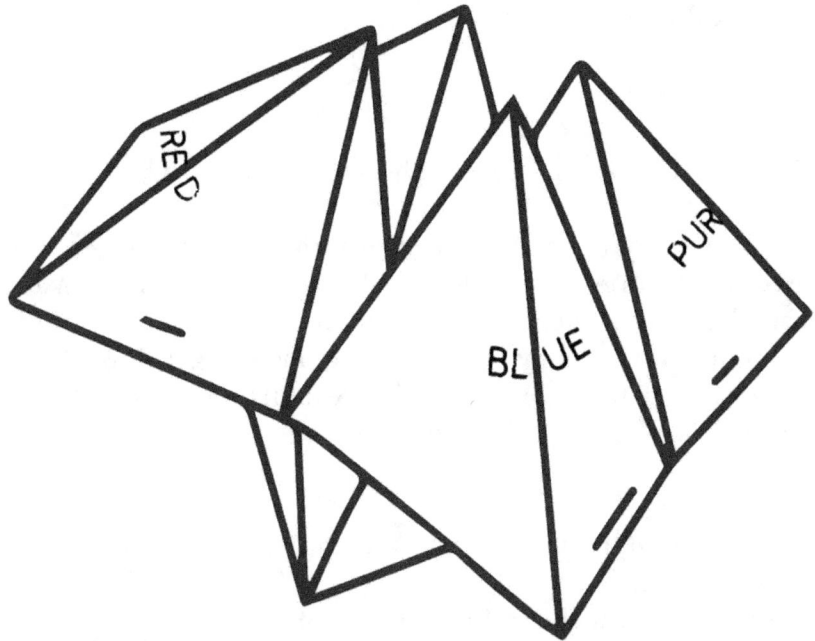

**FIGURE B.12** An example of a Decider Origami.

## Activity B13: Labyrinth

*Level*: Advanced

*Tool for the SEL Toolbox:* Labyrinth

*Objective:* Labyrinths are maze-like formations that have been used for centuries by people to feel more centered and relaxed. The objective of the handheld labyrinth is to create the same sensation, in which, by slowly tracing one's finger through the labyrinth's pathway, a student's breathing may slow down, helping them feel more at ease.

*Materials needed:*
- labyrinth stencils (found at craft stores or online),
- markers,
- white school glue in squeeze containers,
- colored sand,
- heavy cardstock paper or wooden blocks, one per student; the size should be big enough for the chosen stencils,
    OR
- copies of the provided labyrinth, one per student.

*Note:* If using a labyrinth printed onto cardstock, go over the steps on how to use it and allow students to practice for a few minutes.

**Steps for making and using the Labyrinth (with students):**

1. Distribute one piece of cardstock paper (or block) and stencil to each student.
2. Instruct students to place the stencil on the cardstock (or block) and color in the areas allowed by the stencil with a marker. Collect the stencils.
3. Have students carefully squeeze glue onto the colored curvy lines just made from the stencil. Remind students to create lines using only a little glue; doing this will allow the sand to stick better.

4. After the stencil lines have been covered with glue, allow students to sprinkle their chosen color of sand onto the glue sections. Assist students who need help.
5. Allow the glue with the sand to dry; refer to the glue container's instructions regarding the recommended drying time.
6. Once dried, have students gently tap their labyrinths over a garbage can to remove extra sand.
7. Go over steps for how to use a labyrinth, allowing students to practice for a few minutes. Say,
   a) *Place the labyrinth in front of you either on the desk, on your lap, or hold it up with your hand.*
   b) *Place a finger into one of the openings on the labyrinth. Then, very slowly, trace the created pathway with your finger between the lines of the Labyrinth.*
   c) *Remember to slowly trace your finger on it while taking slow breaths.*

   *Note:* Students can use either hand to follow the pathway between the lines. Some people prefer to use their non-dominant hand; doing this can help balance the right and left hemispheres of the brain.
8. Ask students to place their Labyrinths into their SEL Toolboxes after their practice.

---

How the Labyrinth can be used as an SEL Tool:

Students can trace the created pathways with one finger between the lines of the Labyrinths when using the SEL Toolbox Area for a set time. Remind students to slowly trace their fingers while taking slow breaths.

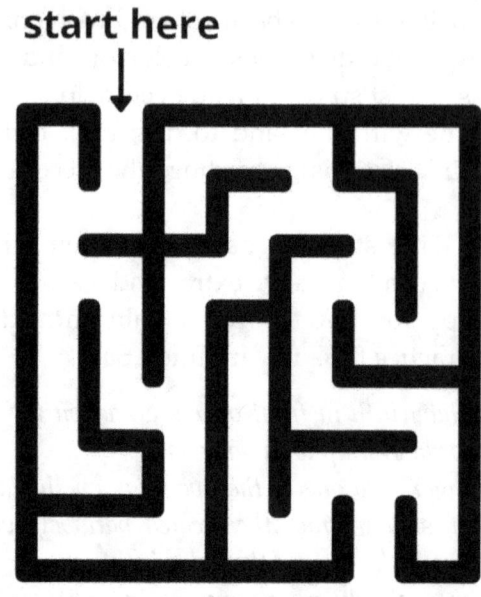

**FIGURE B.13** Two Labyrinth examples.

Copyright material from Lori A. Reichel (2025), *Tactile Tools for Social Emotional Learning*, Routledge

## Activity B14: Laughter Tool

*Level*: Advanced

*Tool for the SEL Toolbox:* Comic Strips/Copy of Jokes/Other Silly Items

*Objective:* Research tells us that young people laugh around 200 to 300 times a day yet, as they age, they laugh less often (adults laugh about fifteen to twenty [15 to 20] times per day). Yet laughter has so many health benefits including reducing cortisol (a stress hormone), strengthening one's immune system, and increasing feelings of calm. The Laughter Tool's purpose is to help students smile and laugh to experience these health benefits.

*Note:* The teacher or the students can provide silly photos, jokes, and/or comic strips to place into the SEL Toolbox Area.

*Materials needed:*
- a variety of appropriate visuals that help students laugh including jokes, comic strips, and silly photos.

**Steps for making and using the Laughter Tool (with students):**

1. Discuss with students how laughing is healthy for people's bodies. Explain that to support laughter, students can place certain appropriate items into their SEL Toolboxes. Provide examples of items that are considered appropriate.
2. Explain what makes the items appropriate. Overall, an appropriate item *does not offend another person (hurt another person's feelings)*.
3. Ask students to bring silly photos, jokes, and/or comic strips to school.
4. If students do not have access to these items, let them find a favorite silly item from any other place, like the library. Make copies of items if allowed.

5. If a photo, joke, or comic strip found by a student cannot be copied, have students try and draw the photo/comic strip and/or write what was written.
6. Allow students to share the silly photos, jokes, and/or comic strips with their peers in small groups.
7. Have students place their Laughter Tools into their SEL Toolboxes.

---

How Laughter Tools can be used as an SEL Tool:

Students can refer to the silly photos and/or read the jokes/comic strips in the SEL Toolbox Area for the set time. Remind students to avoid distracting others when utilizing this tool.

# C

# Tools Dealing With Words

Please remember that some young people are not accustomed to positive vocabulary or writing activities due to unhealthy communication, including violence, in their personal lives. Therefore, allow students time to strengthen their skill sets and provide encouraging feedback when positive words and communications are demonstrated to support their continued use.

## Tips for How to Use the SEL Tools in Section C

Similar to tools provided in other sections, the SEL tools in Section C can be used in the designated SEL Toolbox Area for a set time period. During this time, students should focus on what is written on the chosen tool or complete the writing/reading activity corresponding with the tool.

*Note:* The steps for all activities in Section C include the teacher having discussions on simple concepts relating to the specific tool.

*Please remind students that when utilizing the SEL Toolbox Area, they should remove one SEL Tool from their toolboxes and quietly engage in the corresponding activity for the set time.*

**SEL Tools include:**

C1. Feeling Cards (Beginning)
C2. Gratitude Heart (Beginning)
C3. Personal Support Hand (Beginning)
C4. "I am" Acrostic (Intermediate)
C5. "I feel" Statements (Intermediate)
C6. Positive Reminders on a Stone (Intermediate)
C7. Erasing Thoughts (Advanced)
C8. Inspirational Words (Advanced)
C9. Lessons Learned When Mistakes Happen (Advanced)
C10. Letter to Myself (Advanced)
C11. Lil' Box of Worries (Advanced)
C12. My Little Journal ((Advanced)
C13. Personal Mission Statement (Advanced)
C14. Positive Words For and From Others (Advanced)
C15. Ten (10) Dreams (Advanced)
C16. "Thank You" Note (Advanced)

## Activity C1: Feeling Cards

*Level*: Beginning

*Tool for the SEL Toolbox:* Created Feeling Cards

*Objective:* Recognizing our feelings, including how they affect the way our body feels, is a recommended skill for all people to have. This activity allows students to identify a specific feeling they have and answer simple questions about this feeling. This act of recognizing feelings, including where they are felt in the body and why they might be happening, helps students empower themselves with stronger coping skills.

*Materials needed:*
- five to ten (5 to 10) index cards for each student; Three-by-five-inch (3" × 5") cards work well,
- crayons, colored pencils, markers, or other writing instruments,
- envelopes, one (1) per student,
- Optional: copies of easy-peel stickers with the provided questions listed in Step 4.

**Steps for making and using the Feeling Cards (with students):**

1. Begin by discussing with students the range of feelings people experience. Four (4) common feelings many students can relate to include anger, sadness, fear, and enjoyment (joy).
2. Brainstorm a list of feelings students sometimes experience that may take some time to figure out. Some examples are grumpy, angry, or sad. As students identify feelings, write them on a board. Simple feeling faces can also be drawn by the teacher or a student for each feeling.
3. Distribute the chosen number of index cards to students. Ask students to identify their top three (3) to five (5) unpleasant feelings they sometimes have; these feelings

can be the ones they are most challenged to cope with. Have students draw faces of these feelings onto one side of their index cards, one feeling per card. Students can also write the feeling word onto each card if they have that ability.

4. Have students place the created labels onto the other side of each card or write the following questions on the cards:

    ♦ *What feeling am I feeling?*
    ♦ *Where in my body do I feel this feeling?*
    ♦ *Why might I be feeling this feeling?*
    ♦ *How can I cope with this feeling in a healthy way?*

5. Discuss the provided questions, reminding students to take their time when figuring out the answers.
    For this discussion, consider providing an example. One example is:
    *Lee has a dog at home who has been sick for a few days. One day at school, Lee was feeling sad.*
    For this example, allow students to process each question:

    ♦ What feeling is Lee feeling? (Possible answer: Sad)
    ♦ Where in Lee's body might Lee feel this feeling? (Possible answers: in the heart area, in the shoulders)
    ♦ Why might Lee be feeling this feeling? (Possible answer: Because Lee's dog has been sick.)
    ♦ How can Lee cope with this feeling in a healthy way? (Possible answers: Lee can cry, Lee can talk to the teacher.)

6. If time allows, students can practice answering the questions for one of their feeling cards, sharing their answers with a neighbor.

7. Distribute the envelopes and have students place all their created Feeling Cards into their envelopes. Then have students place the envelopes with the cards into their SEL Toolboxes.

How the Feeling Cards can be used as an SEL Tool:

In the SEL Toolbox Area with the set timer:

- ♦ Students can go through their Feeling Cards and choose the one card/feeling that best identifies the feeling they are experiencing. The student can then answer the questions on the back of the card to further explore the feelings in their bodies and figure out how to cope.
- ♦ If they can, students can write their answers to the provided questions on the blank paper kept in their Toolboxes (as recommended in the Introductory Section).

Students can also display one of their Feeling Cards at their desks to allow others to know how they are feeling.

In addition, the teacher can refer to the Feeling Cards when conflicts occur between students and/or when referring to challenging situations in class readings.

## On the back of feeling cards:

- What feeling am I feeling?
- Where in my body do I feel this feeling?
- Why might I be feeling this feeling?
- How can I cope with this feeling in a healthy way?

**FIGURE C.1** Feeling Card examples.

## Activity C2: Gratitude Heart

*Level*: Beginning

*Tool for the SEL Toolbox:* Gratitude Heart

*Objective:* Research reveals that people who regularly identify what they are grateful for are happier and more optimistic. This activity, recognizing gratitude, supports this practice in which students identify simple things they are grateful for.

*Materials needed:*
- pieces of paper cut into heart shapes, a few for each student,
- crayons, colored pencils, markers, or other writing instruments,
- envelopes, one (1) per student,
- Optional: copies of the provided Heart templates.

**Steps for making the Gratitude Heart (with students):**

1. Begin the activity by defining the word "gratitude" and having a short discussion on this word. One definition of "gratitude" is: *feeling thankful or appreciative of something; feeling grateful.*
2. Provide examples or ask students to provide examples of what a young person may feel grateful about. Examples may include:
    - a specific person in their life, like a family member.
    - spending time at a beach or park.
    - funny jokes.
    - snuggling with a pet.
    - having food to eat.
3. Distribute the heart-shaped papers to students.
4. Ask students to illustrate (draw) or write what they are grateful for onto their hearts. These "things" may include

people, animals, places, etc. Photos can also be glued onto the heart, if available. The date can also be written.
5. Remember to start with only a few examples at a time in which, if a student requests additional "hearts," more can be provided.
6. Allow students to share items they drew/wrote onto their paper hearts, recognizing that all answers are things students can be grateful for.
7. Distribute envelopes for students to place their "Gratitude Hearts" into. Ask students to write the phrase "My Gratitude Heart" or "What I am grateful for" on the envelopes, if they are able to. Then have students place the envelopes into their SEL Toolboxes.

*Note:* Identifying "things" to be grateful for can be challenging for some children. This is especially true when students have experienced trauma. Therefore, as students are working, circulate among them to assist as needed. For students who are unsure of what to put onto their "hearts," guide them with simple answers; for example, a friend in the classroom, a teacher they relate to, a favorite food, etc. Also, consider connecting with an SEL support person in your school for students.

---

How the Gratitude Heart can be used as an SEL Tool:

In the SEL Toolbox Area with the set timer:

- ♦ Students can read what is written on their Gratitude Hearts to be reminded of what they are grateful for.
- ♦ Students can add more things onto their Gratitude Hearts. If their "hearts" are full due to so many things being written, other blank Gratitude Hearts can be completed.

The teacher can also create a "class" Gratitude Heart that can be displayed in the classroom.

**FIGURE C.2** Heart templates for creating gratitude lists.

Copyright material from Lori A. Reichel (2025), *Tactile Tools for Social Emotional Learning*, Routledge

## Activity C3: Personal Support Hand

*Level*: Beginning

*Tool for the SEL Toolbox:* Personal Support Hand

*Objective:* All of us need people in our lives whom we can depend on in an emergency, crisis, or struggle. This activity helps students identify specific people in their own lives they can turn to during times of need.

*Materials needed:*
- pieces of blank paper, one (1) per student,
- pens/pencils/markers,
- Optional: copies of the Personal Support Hand.

**Steps for making the Personal Support Hand (with students):**

1. Define the phrase "support people." A simple definition is: *People in your life who genuinely care for you, can listen to you when you feel uncomfortable or upset, and help you when you need help. These are people we can trust.*
2. Define the term "trust." A simple definition is: *reliable and/or consistent.*
3. Discuss how getting help from others is brave and something everyone needs to do sometimes. Share the thought that willingness to get help from a trusted person is an important trait.
4. Brainstorm a list of trusted people and places young people can approach when they need help. Examples may include a teacher, the principal, a trusted coach, a grandparent, and the local police department (calling 9-1-1).
5. Provide students with a piece of paper and have students trace their non-dominant hand onto it. In the middle of the hand, in the palm area, have students write their names.

    *Note*: Copies of the Personal Support Hand can also be used.

6. Explain that for each finger of their traced hands students are to consider people and places they can trust and go to when in an emergency or needing help. They should then draw something representing these trusted people and places, one person/place for each finger (or write the names of these people/places).
7. Encourage students to be as specific as possible, identifying a person's actual name or how they are referred to. Examples could be, my Godparent Aunt Ying, my PE teacher Mr. Klein, and my friend, Shawn.
8. Provide help to those students who seem to struggle with identifying possible trusted adults and places. For example, discuss with students that in the school setting the school nurse, a specific teacher, or an administrator can be considered an option.
9. Remind students that when they feel uncomfortable, going to the trusted person/place noted on their "hand" is a healthy tool to use. Also, explain that their name in the middle of their "hand" is to remind them that they are special and important.
10. Have students place their completed "hands" into their SEL Toolboxes.

---

How the Personal Support Hand can be used as an SEL Tool:

In the SEL Toolbox Area with the set timer:

- ♦ Students can glance at their list of support people/places to be reminded of who/what is there for them in times of need.
- ♦ Students can update the people and places on their Personal Support Hands.
- ♦ Students can write a letter to one of the people/places.
- ♦ Students can speak with the person (or go to the place if possible) if given permission.

**Directions:**
1. Write your name in the palm area of the hand.
2. On each finger draw or write the names of trusted people who can help you.

**FIGURE C.3** Example of a Personal Support Hand template.

# Activity C4: "I am" Acrostic

*Level*: Intermediate

*Tool for the SEL Toolbox:* Personal "I am" Acrostic

*Objective:* An acrostic is the composition of words or phrases in which each letter of a chosen word forms its own word or phrase. The "I am" acrostic uses a student's name to create this composition in which positive words or phrases referring to the student are written for each letter. The purpose behind the "I am" acrostic is to allow students to identify positive qualities about themselves. This act, of noting positive qualities, supports healthy self-awareness.

*Materials needed:*
- paper for each student,
- crayons, colored pencils, markers, or other writing instruments.

**Steps for making the "I am" Acrostic (with students):**

1. Begin this tool activity by having a discussion with students on what "positive words" and "positive phrases" are about. A basic explanation is *words that are kind and healthy.*
A list of positive words/phrases can also be brainstormed and written on a board.
2. Distribute a piece of paper to each student.
3. Ask students to write "I am" on the top of the paper in large letters (about an inch in height/width).
4. Ask students to write the letters of their names vertically down underneath the "I am" (about an inch in height/width).
5. Using each letter of their name, have students think of positive adjectives or statements that describe who they are and then write these words on the paper with each corresponding letter. Also, inform students that letters of a

name do not have to start with the adjectives/statements, yet can instead be used anywhere in the actual word(s), as shown in the example.
6. If time allows, have students share their completed acrostics.
7. Have students place their completed "I am" acrostics into their SEL Toolboxes.

*Note:* Thinking of positive adjectives for oneself can be challenging for some children. This is especially true when the students have experienced trauma. As students are working, circulate among the students to assist as needed. For students who are unsure of what words/phrases to use, guide them with simple answers like fun, creative, and helpful. Also, consider connecting with an SEL support person in your school for students when needed.

---

How the "I am" Acrostic can be used as an SEL Tool:

In the SEL Toolbox Area with the set timer:

- Students can read their "I am" acrostic when they need to be reminded of who they are. For this, students can be directed to focus on each word/phrase, taking a slow breath for each word/phrase.
- Students can update their "I am" acrostic with new words/phrases or create new acrostics.

I am...

Motivated

Artistic

Trustworthy

Energetic

strOng

**FIGURE C.4** Example of an acrostic for the name Mateo.

## Activity C5: "I feel" Statements

*Level*: Intermediate

*Tool for the SEL Toolbox*: "I feel" Statement worksheets, completed and blank

*Objective:* Learning how to express our feelings in healthy ways is important for maintaining relationships and supports social and emotional learning. This activity provides students the skill of creating "I feel" statements that can be used for expressing uncomfortable feelings to another person.

Due to the differing abilities of students, three (3) versions of "I feel" statements are provided: two basic statements with two (2) fill-in areas and a more advanced statement with three (3) fill-in areas.

*Materials needed:*
- copies of the "I feel" statement (two simpler + one more advanced statements are provided),
- crayons, colored pencils, markers, or other writing instruments,
- an age-appropriate Feelings worksheet found online; this worksheet would display a variety of feelings commonly felt by the age group (your school counselors may have worksheets to use).

**Steps for making and using "I feel" Statements (with students):**

1. Review common feeling words by completing one or both of the following activities:

   a) Display the feelings worksheet found online and have students identify each feeling shown. Students can do this as a group, with a partner, or individually. A copy of the Feelings worksheet sheet can also be placed in the students' SEL Toolboxes.

b) Play "Feeling Charades." To play, separate the different feelings shown on a feelings worksheet in which only one feeling is found on each piece of paper. Let the students who volunteer pick one of the pieces of paper (one feeling) at a time to act out the noted feeling while their peers attempt to identify it.

*Note:* The skill of *knowing* how one feels may be simple for some students, but some others may struggle to identify their feelings. Therefore, it is recommended a simple feeling word activity be completed. In addition, a feeling worksheet can be provided for students to point to pictures for how they are feeling. This feeling worksheet can be displayed on a classroom wall or copied to be placed into students' SEL Toolboxes.

2. Explain how feelings shared with others is important for our relationships; a statement like *"we want our words to be helpful, not hurtful"* could be used.
Another example is to say:
*We are going to practice using "I feel" sentences when we have an unpleasant feeling. Saying "I feel" words to one another can help us better understand how a person is feeling and is a kinder way of sharing our feelings.*

3. Display the following statement to the students. (Either show the created prompts or write them on a board.)

"I feel _____ when (or because)_____."

4. Allow students to practice how to use "I feel" statements by modeling an example for the class. The example should focus on a situation in which a child may have an unpleasant feeling. For example:

*"Imagine Faith is a first grader in our school. One day another student, Lee, cuts in front of Faith in the cafeteria line without asking. How might Faith be feeling?"*

Answers might include sad, angry, frustrated, and upset.

5. Fill in the "I feel" statement choosing one of the stated feelings from the example. Ask students to provide a reason for why Faith might feel that way. Write this

answer after the "when" or "because" in the blank space.

Depending upon the student's abilities, the "I need (or want)" statement can be explained and practiced. This part of the statement requires stating what the person wants or needs to feel heard. For the above example, a complete "I feel" statement for Faith may read:

*"I feel sad when Lee cuts in front of me without asking.*
*I need Lee to ask me first."*

6. Distribute copies of the "I feel" statement, one for each student. Ask students to choose one of the feelings noted on the Feelings worksheet and fill in the blanks with an example of one time they felt that emotion. Ask students to share one of their statements with their classmates. This can also be done as a "Think, Pair, Share" activity.
7. Make sure to inform students that when an "I feel" statement is shared, all they need to do is listen; they can also say, *"Thank you for letting me know how you feel."*
8. Have students place their "I feel" statements (and emotions worksheets) into their SEL Toolboxes. Also, include blank "I feel' worksheets for future use.

How "I feel" Statements can be used as an SEL Tool:

In the SEL Toolbox Area with the set timer:

- ♦ Students can write "I feel" statements on the provided worksheets or on blank paper for how they are currently feeling.
- ♦ Students can read their previously created "I feel" statements.

Also:

- ♦ "I feel" statements can be further practiced during classroom book discussions, especially when stories of conflict are told. During these times students can be reminded of how "I feel" statements support healthier communication between people.
- ♦ Students can be directed to their SEL Toolboxes and "I feel" statement worksheets when conflicts arise in the classroom.

I feel _____ when _____.

OR

I feel _____ because _____.

**FIGURE C.5.1** Two types of "I feel" statements for younger students to practice.

I feel _____

when/because

_____.

I need (or want)

_____

_____.

**FIGURE C.5.2** Advanced "I feel" statement for older students.

## Activity C6: Positive Reminders on a Stone

*Level*: Intermediate

*Tool for the SEL Toolbox:* Stone with a Positive Word

*Objective:* Often we can become calmer and more centered when focusing on a specific positive word that we connect with. For example, the word "hope" reminds some people to have hope in the present and future moments. This activity allows students to create simple stone reminders that they can refer to when wanting to focus on positive words.

*Materials needed:*
- One (1) stone per student; these can be purchased at an "arts and crafts" store or found at a local beach/park,
- different colors of paint (remember to check for healthy and safe brands of paint to use),
- permanent markers in a variety of colors,
- a timer set to a specific duration for students to focus on their positive reminders.

**Steps for making the Positive Reminders on a Stone (with students):**

1. Ask students to define the word "positive." A simple definition is *friendly, supportive, and/or helpful.*
2. Ask students to choose a stone and paint it with their favorite color or a color that helps remind them of something positive.
3. As the paint is drying, brainstorm a group of words that remind students to be positive. This list can be written on a board. Sample words include *peace, hope, love, and kindness.*
4. After the paint dries, have each student write in LARGE LETTERS their chosen word onto their stone.

5. Have students sit comfortably and either place their stones on a table in front of them, with the word facing them, or students can hold onto the stones so they can see their words. Then have the class practice taking three (3) to five (5) slow breaths while focusing on their chosen words. Set the timer if needed.
6. Have students place their stones with their chosen words into their SEL Toolboxes.

---

How the Positive Reminders on a Stone can be used as an SEL Tool:

In the SEL Toolbox Area with the set timer:

- ♦ Students can sit with their stones, holding them for a few moments.
- ♦ As students hold their stones, they can practice a simple breathing exercise.

Students can also keep their stones at their desks to refer to during the school day.

## Activity C7: Erasing Thoughts

*Level*: Advanced

*Tool for the SEL Toolbox:* Small Whiteboard with Whiteboard Marker/Eraser

*Objective:* Writing down what we are thinking and feeling is often cathartic to many people. In addition, slowly erasing what is written can help release these thoughts/feelings. This activity allows students to express their thoughts/feelings and then "erase" them.

*Materials needed:*
- a small whiteboard for each student (can be found online or at dollar stores),
- a whiteboard marker for each student,
- a whiteboard eraser or rag (old t-shirts can be cut into small rags for erasing whiteboards).
- Optional: One classroom whiteboard, marker, and eraser may be used; this would be stored in the SEL Toolbox Area.

**Steps for using the Small Whiteboard Tool (with students):**

1. Discuss with students about how writing down our thoughts and feelings can often help people feel better. This includes slowly erasing our thoughts/feelings after writing them down.
2. Distribute the small whiteboards, markers, and erasers to students.
3. Ask students to practice writing about their thoughts and feelings. After a minute, ask everyone to erase slowly what they had written. The speed of erasing can be different for individual students yet encourage them to use the eraser slowly and calmly.

4. Allow students to share how they feel about writing and then erasing their words. Recognize that some students may have the ability to write more words and to keep them in a journal. For these students, refer to the "My Little Journal" activity.
5. Have students place their boards, markers, and erasers into their SEL Toolboxes.

---

How the Small Whiteboard can be used as an SEL Tool:

- ♦ Students can write and slowly erase their words on their whiteboards in the SEL Toolbox Area for a set time.
- ♦ The teacher can model this activity by allowing the whole class to list thoughts/feelings they currently have, in which the words are then slowly erased in front of the students.
- ♦ The boards may also be used for "doodling." Research has found that drawing and doodling have many health benefits.

## Activity C8: Inspirational Words

*Level*: Advanced

*Tool for the SEL Toolbox:* Hard copies of Inspirational Words or Individual "CDs" with added QR Codes

*Objective:* Reading certain inspirational words can help a person feel more positive; so can hearing certain melodies and/or someone reading a poem or making a speech. This activity allows each student to identify their favorite sayings, songs, scripture, poems, etc., that, when read or heard, increase the students' positive and happy feelings.

*Materials needed:*
- access to age-appropriate sayings, songs, scripture, poems, or other inspirational words,
- cardstock paper for printing the chosen items (either by a computer printer or by hand),
- crayons, colored pencils, markers, or other writing instruments.
- Optional items:
    a) tablets/computers with access to the Internet,
    b) access to an online QR Code maker,
    c) a "cd" or "record" outline template (an example is provided),
    d) earbuds/headphones for listening to items.

*Note:* The provided sample "CD" image was used in a former course of the author. To create individual "CDs," each student made up to four (4) different QR Codes referring to a variety of inspirational media sources which were digitally placed on the "CD" template. Their final product was then placed into their SEL Toolboxes.

**Steps for making Inspirational Words (with students):**

1. Discuss with students how people sometimes feel more positive when they read or hear certain sayings, songs, poems, etc. For example, hearing the song "You Got a Friend in Me" by Randy Newman, the theme song from the movie *Toy Story*, puts a smile on some young people's faces.
2. Allow each student to think of a handful of sayings, songs, poems, etc., that help them feel more positive. If available and allowed, students can look up appropriate items online. This research can also be completed at home or during free time.
3. Upon finding their sayings/songs/ poems/etc., have students make a hard copy of each, which includes printing the actual words from an online source or writing them onto a piece of paper.
   Optional: If you are allowing students to create a "CD" with QR codes, provide students time for online access through a tablet or computer to find their items and create their QR codes. A simple free QR Code Generator is found at: https://www.qrcode-monkey.com/. Upon creating QR codes, each code can be copied or pasted onto a "CD" image which would then be printed onto the cardstock.
4. Have students place the hard copy of their chosen Inspirational Words into their SEL Toolboxes.

---

How Inspirational Words can be used as an SEL Tool:

In the SEL Toolbox Area with the set timer:

- ♦ Students can read or listen to their chosen Inspirational Words.
- ♦ Students can quietly read their Inspirational Words aloud. Sometimes saying words aloud helps children connect to what the words mean to them.

Also, the teacher can read and/or play examples of Inspirational Words when needed/wanted.

**FIGURE C.8** A CD template example.

## Activity C9: Lessons Learned When Mistakes Happen

*Level*: Advanced

*Tool for the SEL Toolbox:* Lesson Learned Written on Small Paper

*Objective:* Oftentimes young people focus on the mistakes they make, failing to understand that everyone makes them. Making mistakes is actually an important part of learning. Helping students practice "learning from mistakes" supports healthy self-regulation skills aligning with a growth mindset. Therefore, this activity allows students to focus on the lessons learned from a mistake while "tossing" the mistake away.

*Materials needed:*
- a piece of paper for each student, a six-inch square (6 x 6); the paper can be scrap paper also,
- crayons, colored pencils, markers, or other writing instruments.

**Steps for making and using the Lesson Learned Tool (with students):**

1. Define the word "mistake." A simple definition is *an action or decision wrongly made that creates an unwanted or unintended outcome.*
2. Provide examples of possible mistakes that are typical for the age group. Examples may include:
   - saying an unkind word to another person or pet,
   - not telling the truth about something,
   - betraying someone's trust in you.
3. Distribute a piece of paper to each student.
4. Ask each student to carefully rip the piece of paper into two pieces, almost equal in size.

5. Ask students to write on one of the pieces of paper a mistake they had made. Explain that no names are needed on their paper, but only the mistakes they made should be written.
6. Refer to the other piece of paper and ask students to write the words "What I learned" onto the paper. Ask them to reflect on what they learned from the mistake they made and write that on the paper. For example, if they said an unkind word to another person, they might have learned: *My words can hurt others and sometimes I need to pause before speaking.*
7. Allow students to talk with others in the classroom if they are unsure of what they learned from a mistake. This can be done one-on-one with a teacher or peer, or as an overall class discussion.
8. Have students place the pieces of paper with what they learned into their SEL Toolboxes. Also, provide additional pieces of small paper for future mistakes students may make. Remind students they can refer to both when choosing to use the SEL Toolbox Area with the set timer.
9. To finish the activity, ask students to crumple up their mistake – in other words, have students crumple up the piece of paper with their mistake written on it. Then:
    a) ask students to throw it into a recycling bin
       OR
    b) ask students to throw the mistakes paper at the teacher after counting to "three" (3). For this activity, count to three (3) out loud in which students will throw their "mistakes" at the teacher; remember to step into a safe area and cover your eyes for protection. Choosing to complete the activity in this manner increases the level of recollection for students ("I threw my mistake at Ms. R.!").

How the Lesson Learned Tool can be used as an SEL Tool:

In the SEL Toolbox Area with the set timer:

- ♦ Students can refer to their past lessons to remind themselves everyone makes mistakes from which lessons are learned.
- ♦ After recognizing they made a mistake, students can get a blank piece of paper from their Toolbox and, after ripping it in half, write their mistake on one piece and their lesson learned on the other. The "mistake" can then be tossed into a recycling bin and the lesson learned placed into the Toolbox.

This Lesson Learned activity can be further practiced during classroom discussions when the teacher recognizes a mistake was made or when stories on mistakes arise. During these times students can be reminded of how focusing on the lessons they learned helps them grow and that everyone makes mistakes. This is an example of having a growth mindset.

## Activity C10: Letter to Myself

*Level*: Advanced

*Tool for the SEL Toolbox:* Completed Letter to Oneself

*Objective:* Some teachers ask students to write letters to themselves and then collect them for students to receive back at a later time. The purpose behind doing this is to provide young people the opportunity to reflect on their personal growth. For example: When the author taught middle school, some of her former students wrote letters to themselves that they received back in their 12th-grade health education class. The 12th-grade health education teacher, Mrs. V., shared how students enjoyed reflecting on their growth over the years. This activity provides younger students with the same opportunity in which, after answering a variety of questions, they return to their written letters later to remind themselves what was written, as well as reflect on their recent growth.

*Materials needed:*
- copies of the "Letter to Myself" or a list of similar questions for students to answer on a worksheet, one per student,
- pens/pencils,
- envelopes, one (1) per student.

**Steps for making the Letter to Myself (with students):**

1. Explain to students that they will be writing a letter to themselves that will be put into their Toolboxes. Note that the purpose of this letter is to remind them of their strengths and talents, as well as their values and dreams.
2. Have a simple discussion on letter writing and/or the definitions of some of the noted terms.

3. Distribute the provided worksheet and ask students to complete the worksheet.

    Students can also complete the worksheet at home to be brought back to the classroom.
4. Provide envelopes for students to place their letters into. On the outside of the envelopes have students write something like "My Letter to Me" and the date. Have them place their letters in the envelopes and then put them into their SEL Toolboxes.

---

How the Letter to Myself can be used as an SEL Tool:

In the SEL Toolbox Area with the set timer:

- ♦ Students can read their letters to themselves; they may choose to read these letters aloud quietly. Sometimes saying words aloud helps children connect to what the words mean to them.
- ♦ Students can update their letters with new answers. If choosing to update answers, ask students to leave their former answers visible so they can have a list of their former thoughts as well.

The teacher can also save letters written at a specific time to be shared with students in future years/grades.

## Letter to Myself

Dear _____,                    Date: _____

Hello me!

A. My favorite thing about myself is:

B. Two adjectives that best describe me include:

C. My favorite hobby/sport/activity is:

D. When I feel overwhelmed or anxious, I do the following to help me relax:

E. Music that puts a smile on my face includes:

F. Over the next year I hope to do the following:

G. I choose the following decision to make sure I stay healthy:

H. When I need to talk with someone or want support, I talk with _____ because:

Remember to stay strong and be the best "YOU" you can be!

                                        Love, Your Best Friend (Me),

                                        _____

**FIGURE C.10** Template of the "Letter to Myself."

## Activity C11: Lil' Box of Worries

*Level*: Advanced

*Tool for the SEL Toolbox:* Lil' Box of Worries with Papers Inside

*Objective:* Writing down our thoughts and feelings helps us to process what we are thinking/feeling. Writing can also help us return to thoughts at a later time. This activity allows students to write down something they are worried or anxious about and then place their worries inside their "Worry Boxes." The act of "placing our worries" into a box represents how we sometimes need to focus on other things and then return later to our worries to resolve them.

*Materials needed:*
- small boxes, like earring or necklace boxes, one (1) for each student,
- markers/pens for writing on the box,
- small pieces of paper to put inside the boxes,
- address labels with positive reminders written on them; for example:
- *I am enough. I belong. I am strong. I am useful.*
- Optional: stickers to place onto the box.

**Steps for making and using the Lil' Box of Worries (with students):**

1. Discuss with students that sometimes people have thoughts that distract them from daily chores or events; these thoughts can cause them to worry. Share a simple definition of worry, like *thoughts that cause concern or anxiety.*
Remind students that people of all ages worry about something at times; this is a natural occurrence. Yet sometimes we need to put our worries away to focus on other things (or to get rid of them).
2. Provide a box and markers/pens to each student. Ask students to write "My Worry Box" or something similar

onto the box. Students can also decorate the box with materials like stickers if available.
3. Distribute small pieces of papers to each student, asking them to put them into their boxes. Students can choose how many they want – five (5) to twelve (12) pieces usually work.
4. Distribute the pre-made labels to students to stick onto their boxes (on the top or bottom).
One example of what can be written on the labels is:
*I am enough. I belong. I am strong. I am useful.*
5. Explain the following by saying:
*Sometimes we get concerned and worried about something, especially when things are out of our control. When this happens, please write down your concern or worry on one of these pieces of paper and place it in your "Lil Box of Worries." Doing this can help us put our worries aside so we can focus on other things.*
6. Continue to explain that after their concern/worry is placed into the box, they should read the label to themselves. Allow students to discuss what the saying means to them.
7. Have students place their "Lil' Boxes of Worries" into their SEL Toolboxes.

---

How the Lil' Box of Worries can be used as an SEL Tool:

♦ Students can write down their worries on the small pieces of paper and place them into the "Lil' Box of Worries" when using the SEL Toolbox Area for a set time.

♦ The teacher can model this activity if sensing students are anxious or worried about something. For example, when students need to complete a state exam. In this instance, the teacher can provide students with the opportunity to create a list of their worries on little pieces of paper that can later be placed into the teacher's Lil' Box of Worries.

**FIGURE C.11** Example of a Lil' Box of Worries with a label.

## Activity C12: My Little Journal

*Level*: Advanced

*Tool for the SEL Toolbox:* Created Journal

*Objective:* Writing down what we are thinking and/or feeling is often cathartic to many people. Used as a coping skill, this act also helps young people self-regulate their emotions. Therefore, this activity includes students creating their own journals to write their thoughts and/or feelings into.

*Materials needed:*
- at least five (5) pieces of paper for each student; typical paper, eight (8) inches by eleven (11) inches, works well and can be cut in half to create more pages for a smaller journal,
- safety scissors for cutting papers in half,
- staplers,
- pens/pencils,
- a timer set to your specified time for students to write their journals.

**Steps for making and using My Little Journal (with students):**

1. Discuss with students how some people like to write in a journal regularly. Allow students to consider what could be written in a journal. Answers include daily events, exciting things, problems that have occurred during the day, and the emotions they experienced.
2. Distribute five (5) pieces of paper to students, explaining that each student will be creating their own journal.
3. Have students carefully fold the papers in half, creating a crease at the center of the papers. Have everyone cut their papers in half with the safety scissors; papers may need to be cut one at a time.

4. Ask students to pile these pages together to form a little book, stapling one side of the book to keep all pages together. If using five (5) pieces, it will total ten (10) pages. Teachers may choose to staple the little journals for students.
5. Have students design covers for their journals, writing something like "My Little Journal" or "My Thoughts/Feelings" on the cover.
6. Explain to students that the created journals will now serve as a place for them to write their thoughts/feelings.
7. Set a timer for five (5) minutes and ask students to write about their current thoughts and feelings in their journals. Afterward, students may choose to share how they felt when writing during that period or share what they wrote (if they want to).
8. Have students place the hard copies of their Little Journals into their SEL Toolboxes.

---

How My Little Journal can be used as an SEL Tool:

In the SEL Toolbox Area with the set timer:

- ♦ Students can write or draw in their journals.
- ♦ Students can read what was previously written/drawn in their journals.

## Activity C13: Personal Mission Statement

*Level*: Advanced

*Tool for the SEL Toolbox:* Personal Mission Statement

*Objective:* Reminding ourselves of the positive qualities we possess or what we believe our purpose is can help us feel more grounded and centered when we feel distressed. This activity of creating a Mission Statement helps students identify their positive qualities as well as what they believe their purposes are.

*Note:* Students can also complete this activity outside the classroom. The final statement can be brought back to the classroom and shared/stored in the SEL Toolbox.

*Materials needed:*
- pieces of paper, one (1) for each student,
- pens/pencils,
  OR
- use of a computer/laptop/tablet for each student so that final mission statements can be printed on cardstock/paper,
- a timer set to your chosen amount of time.

**Steps for making the Personal Mission Statement (with students):**

1. Begin by defining the phrase "mission statement" and having a brief discussion on why people and businesses often create mission statements.
   Mission statements are typically created by people and businesses to identify what is important to them and/or their purpose. These statements can be one or two sentences reminding the writer(s) of their values.
2. Other words/phrases that can be defined include:
   a) purpose: *a personal and meaningful belief for why something exists or hopes to accomplish*

b) positive qualities: *personal aspects, strengths, character traits, and/or skills that a person considers healthy or helps them/others in some way*

3. Provide examples of personal mission statements. Here are two:

    *I strive to live a life that demonstrates care and appreciation for everyone. I believe in helping all people, including those less fortunate than myself.*

    *I commit to my education because I believe what I learn will help me and others.*

4. Distribute a piece of paper to each student or ask everyone to open their writing programs on their computers/laptops/tablets.
5. Provide at least five (5) minutes for students to write one or two statements that could reflect their mission statement.
6. Ask for volunteers to read their mission statements aloud but remember that students have the right to "pass."
7. Have students place their Mission Statements into their SEL Toolboxes.

---

How the Personal Mission Statement can be used as an SEL Tool:

- ♦ Students can read their Mission Statements in the SEL Toolbox Area with the set timer. This reading can be completed aloud if quiet voices are used. Remember, sometimes saying words aloud helps children connect to what the words mean to them.
- ♦ The teacher can model how to create a Mission Statement by leading a discussion and creating an overall Classroom Mission Statement.

## Activity C14: Positive Words For and From Others

*Level*: Advanced

*Tool for the SEL Toolbox:* The Completed List of Positive Words from Others

*Objective:* Who doesn't like to receive kind words from others? Most of us do. This activity allows students to write kind words to one another, supporting positive social learning. In addition, healthy hormones are released in our bodies when performing a positive deed for another or when we are the recipient of a nice deed. Therefore, this activity also supports feeling healthy emotions.

*Materials needed:*
- paper for each student,
- pens/pencils/ markers for writing,
- timer.

*Notes:*
- Depending upon the size of the class, students can be divided into smaller groups or work as a whole class to complete the activity.
- The author recommends the completed papers be collected by the teacher to ensure all comments are positive before the students receive them.
- The teacher should also add positive comments to each student's paper.

**Steps for making Positive Words For and From Others (with students):**

1. Have students sit in a circle or any other organized formation. Sitting in a circle is suggested because a circle helps to keep papers organized when they are passed between students.

2. Discuss what the phrase "positive comments" means. For example: *positive comments are statements/sentences a person says that are complimentary and genuine (real).*
3. Remind students that a person can give other people and themselves positive comments.
4. Brainstorm examples of positive comments with students. Some include:

*To another student:*
*I really appreciated when you helped me with my math worksheet.*
*You have a nice smile.*
*You have a nice singing voice.*
*You were brave when you stood up to the person teasing me.*
*To oneself:*
*I try my best when I do math.*
*I am brave and ask for help when I need or want it.*

5. Explain to students that positive comments are best when they refer to the personality or acts of a person, not what the person looks like or owns.
6. Give each student in the group a piece of paper. Have each student write their name clearly on top of the paper.
7. Set the timer for a specific time (one or two (1 or 2) minutes usually works). Then ask students to pass their papers with their names on top to the students to the right of them. Once everyone has another student's paper, start the timer and ask everyone to think of one positive comment for the student whose name is on the top. After deciding on one positive comment, ask the students to write them down.
8. Students should also write their names next to the positive comment they wrote.
9. Once the timer goes off, circulate the papers again and reset the timer.
10. Continue until all students in the class (group) have an opportunity to write something for each student.

11. Collect the completed papers and inform students that a final comment will be written on all papers by the teacher which is why they are being collected. Each paper will then be placed into their individual SEL Toolboxes for students to read at a future time.

---

How the Positive Words For and From Others can be used as an SEL Tool:

Students can read the positive comments written by their peers and teacher when in the SEL Toolbox Area for a set time.

## Activity C15: Ten (10) Dreams

*Level*: Advanced

*Tool for the SEL Toolbox:* List of Ten (10) Dreams

*Objective:* Research tells us that people who identify personal goals or dreams tend to feel more purposeful and/or motivated especially when struggling with life's challenges. This activity allows students to "dream" about goals that they hope to one day experience or reach. Upon reading their created lists, students can be reminded of their dreams especially when feeling unmotivated or upset.

*Note:* This activity can begin as a classroom lesson and then continue at a later time.

*Materials needed:*
- a piece of paper for each student,
- pens/pencils/ markers for writing.

**Steps for making the Ten (10) Dreams (with students):**

1. Begin the activity by discussing what dreams are to people as well as the purpose of dreams (or goals). Basically:
   *A dream is something a person hopes to do or accomplish one day. Another word a person may use for a dream is the word "goal."*
2. Allow for a short discussion on examples of "dreams" students may have. Examples, which can be written on a board, may include:
   - having a pet cat one day,
   - joining a sports team,
   - getting one's ears pierced,
   - traveling to Disney World.

Ensure students understand that their dreams can be about almost anything in their lives including learning, careers, travel, family, fun/adventure, things they would like to own, self-improvement, creating/making/building something, and service to others.
3. Distribute a piece of paper to each student.
4. Ask students to write numbers one (1) to ten (10) down serially on the left side of their papers.
5. Have students begin listing their "dreams" on their papers. Due to this list being a "work-in-progress," inform students they can add additional "dreams" when utilizing the SEL Toolbox Area.
6. Have students place their lists of dreams into their SEL Toolboxes.

---

How the Ten (10) Dreams can be used as an SEL Tool:

In the SEL Toolbox Area with the set timer:

- ♦ Students can read over their completed lists, writing on their papers if a dream/goal was reached.
- ♦ Students can continue to "dream" by adding to their lists.

## Activity C16: "Thank You" Note

*Level*: Advanced

*Tool for the SEL Toolbox:* A Blank "Thank You" Note Card/Paper

*Objective:* Research informs us that completing positive deeds for others helps release healthy hormones for the people performing them, as well as for the people who are recipients of this deed. People who watch these positive acts also have healthy hormones released. This activity supports the release of these healthy hormones, as well as encourages SEL, by allowing students to identify people they want to thank and then write "Thank You" notes for.

*Materials needed:*
- pieces of paper, tablets/computers/laptops, or blank cards for each student,
- pens/pencils/ markers for writing,
- envelopes and stamps (if sending notes through the mail).

**Steps for making the "Thank You" Notes (with students):**

1. Ask students to think of the important people in their lives or people who have done something kind for them. This may be family members, peers, medical professionals, neighbors, etc. Remember to review trusted adults, too, as noted in the Personal Support Hand Activity.
2. Introduce the concept of writing "thank you" notes to people who have been kind to us. Explain that each student will be allowed to write a "thank you" note for one specific person in their lives.
3. Also, share that these notes will be confidential and do not need to be shared with others in the classroom.
4. Review possible items to include in a "thank you" note, including:

a) composing a greeting to the individual (For example: *Dear Dr. Garcia.*);
   b) noting one to two specific reasons why they are thanking the person; and
   c) a signature.

   An example can be created by the whole class and written on a board.
5. Distribute a paper/blank card/etc. to each student. Then ask each student to write a "thank you" note to someone.
6. Collect the finished "thank you" notes and ask each student to obtain the location to which the notes should be sent.
7. Have students send out the "Thank You" notes. For this, students can be taught how to properly address an envelope and send items through the mail. Or, if the recipients are in the school building, the notes can be placed in the appropriate office mailboxes.
8. Have additional cards or papers placed into the SEL Toolboxes for writing future "Thank You" notes.

---

How the "Thank You" Note can be used as an SEL Tool:

Due to the created "Thank You" notes being sent to their recipients, blank "Thank You" notes can be stored in the SEL Toolbox Area. Students can then write new notes when in the SEL Toolbox Area for a set time.

For Product Safety Concerns and Information please contact our EU
representative  GPSR@taylorandfrancis.com
Taylor & Francis Verlag GmbH, Kaufingerstraße 24, 80331 München, Germany

www.ingramcontent.com/pod-product-compliance
Lightning Source LLC
Chambersburg PA
CBHW070402240426
43661CB00056B/2501